THE TALL SHIPS
ARE SAILING

THE TALL SHIPS
ARE SAILING

The Cutty Sark Tall Ships Races

Holly Hollins

Foreword by
Lieutenant-Commander the Honourable
Greville Howard VRD, RNR

DAVID & CHARLES
North Pomfret, Vermont 05053

This book is dedicated to
'Father' and the 'Family':
Lieutenant-Commander the Honourable Greville Howard VRD, RNR,
and the Sail Training Family throughout the world.

The Cutty Sark Tall Ships Races are organised by
The Sail Training Association
5 Mumby Road, Gosport, Hampshire.
Author and publishers owe the Association
a great debt of gratitude for their tireless help
in producing this book

**British Library Cataloguing
in Publication Data**

Hollins, Holly
  The tall ships are sailing.
  1. Tall Ships Race
  I. Title
  797.1'4   GV832
  ISBN 0-7153-8028-1

Printed in Great Britain
by Jolly & Barber Ltd, Rugby
for David & Charles (Publishers) Limited
Brunel House   Newton Abbot   Devon

CONTENTS

Foreword 7
1 The American Sail Training Association Races, 1980 11
2 Kristiansand to Kiel aboard *Sørlandet* 25
3 Arrival at Kiel 35
4 The Parade of Sail 65
5 *Danmark* in the Baltic 75
6 Karlskrona 97
7 Cruise in Company from Karlskrona to Frederikshavn aboard *Kruzenshtern* 115
8 To Amsterdam aboard *Dar Pomorza* 123
9 Sail Amsterdam 149
10 After Amsterdam 159
Appendices 167
Bibliography 183
Acknowledgements 187
Index 189

FOREWORD

I am delighted to write a foreword to this book by Holly Hollins, a ubiquitous and well-liked member of our great international Sail Training Family, for it is remarkable how little the general public knows about us, and it follows that the very readable information in these pages is welcome. It tells the world what we have been doing for over twenty-five years.

The Sail Training movement was the vision of a man called Bernard Morgan who would not take 'no' for an answer. He decided that to get young people to meet in the friendly rivalry of Sail Training races at sea, where they would learn the virtues of co-operation and self-reliance—as in the old sailing-ship saying 'one hand for the ship and one for yourself'—would make them better and therefore happier people. Also, by sharing experiences after the races were over the younger generations of different nations would come to meet each other and make friends.

Experience has proved this to be true. It is out of this enlightened dream that our international 'family' has grown, for, as a Polish writer summed it up: 'the sea is our bridge'.

How has this quiet but substantial success come about? The absence of politics is, I am sure, a big factor for we all know how politics can ruin sport and any attempt to introduce them into the Fleet has always failed because we are dealing with young people of many nations, young people who have already learnt mutual respect through shared experiences at sea and at the wonderfully spontaneous parties that follow the races.

I wish this book the kind of success it deserves and I am sure it will encourage the young people who have not yet experienced belonging to our Family to find out how they can come to join us. If this happens then all Holly's efforts will have been worthwhile.

Greville Howard
Brouch/Mersch, G-D of Luxembourg
June 1981

Course of Race One and area of Race Two

The Norwegian full-rigged ship, *Sørlandet*, owned by the city of Kristiansand, at the Windjammer Parade, Bremerhaven, August 1980 *(Stadthildstelle Seestadt Bremerhaven)*

THE AMERICAN SAIL TRAINING ASSOCIATION RACES, 1980

Who hath desired the sea? —the sight of salt water unbounded,
The heave and the halt and the hurl, and the crash of the comber
wind-hounded?

RUDYARD KIPLING, 'The Sea and the Hills'

At Liverpool Street Station I fell into conversation with a Norwegian whose home was near Kristiansand, and from him I learnt that the sailing ship *Sørlandet*, which I was to join, was looking splendid with new rigging, sails and fresh paintwork. She had been recommissioned after lying idle for over seven years. My excitement was mounting.

We arrived at Kristiansand South at 0100 on 2 July 1980. Lighthouses were flashing as we neared the coast. Gradually, the city appeared from behind the islands and hills, and then we saw the floodlit rigging and masts of two square-riggers, towering above the quays. *Sørlandet* was lying near the Ecuadorian barque *Guayas* which had raced across the North Atlantic from Boston with a small fleet of training vessels, some of which still lay at this attractive harbour: *Lindø*, a topsail schooner from the United States; *Blanca Estela*, a Swan 65 from Chile; *Christian Venturer* from Bermuda, a schooner rigged with junk sails; and *Sabre*, a Nicholson 55, representing Great Britain.

This transatlantic race, and other events earlier in the year at Colombia in South America, were organised by the American Sail Training Association to encourage ships from the Americas to participate in the Cutty Sark International Tall Ships Races in Europe. Barclay H. Warburton III, President of the Association and owner of the brigantine *Black Pearl*, had helped to organise the race. The Chairman of the ASTA is Vice-Admiral Thomas R. Weschler, USN (Retd); the Vice-Chairman, Commander Tylor Field II, USN, was their representative in Kristiansand who greeted the competitors.

THE RACES FROM THE AMERICAS

The ASTA Race series began on 6 May at Cartagena in Colombia, over 5,000 miles from Norway, by the course of the races. And *Blanca Estela* and *Guayas* had had to sail still further to be at the start, as had two training yachts from the British forces, *Chaser* and *Sabre*. This race entailed a complicated passage through the Windward Islands, but fortunately there were fair winds for some of the ships, including *Guayas* and her sister ship *Gloria* from Colombia, as they passed between the islands of Cuba, Haiti and the Dominican Republic. The four-masted topsail schooner *Juan Sebastian de Elcano* from Spain was also competing in Class A for square-riggers of more than 150 tons Thames Measurement and other vessels of 500 tons Thames Measurement and over—selected at the discretion of the committee.

Class B, which may be sub-divided when necessary, encompasses all other sailing vessels with a low limit size of 9.14 metres (30 feet) on the waterline. *Esperanza* and *Fortuna II* of Argentina joined others in this class.

The two British entries, *Chaser*, crewed by the Royal Navy, and *Sabre* by the Royal Armoured Corps and Royal Corps of Signals—both Nicholson 55s from the Joint Services Sailing Centre at Gosport—had cruised in company to Cartagena, changing crews at regular intervals. Major David Scholfield was in command of *Sabre* from Gibraltar to Antigua. In this way a wide range of young people from the forces were able to experience life at sea under a variety of conditions throughout the voyages. During the transatlantic passage, these yachts had remained in sight of one another—a safety precaution which was also a social success. After changing crews in Antigua they sailed for Cartagena where there was a good reception. Apart from the starting line, which proved difficult for the larger vessels, there were no particular problems and the 1,600-mile course was completed at Norfolk, Virginia, nearly two weeks later.

The next stage was the Class B race from Norfolk to Boston, with the Class A ships cruising in company. The American brig *Unicorn*, the brigantines *Young America* (crewed by girl scouts) and *Glad Tidings*, the three-masted topsail schooner *Lindø*, the bermudan ketch *Mabel Stevens*, and the *Pride of Baltimore* joined the fleet there.

The race to Boston was windless in contrast with conditions later across the Atlantic. HMSTY *Sabre* spent two days lying completely becalmed, entertained on one occasion by a small school of whales who laid on a display of belly-flops close by the yacht. These gentle creatures suddenly glide to the surface from the great deep which they know so well. Their knowledge, like that of all sea mammals, is instinctive, natural and not subject to the potential errors of computerised machines. They have some affinity with ships that depend on the force of the wind in the sails; their crews experience the contrasting effects of calms and storms and come to understand the elements. Sailors cannot defeat the elements; they must work with them. They must come to terms with the sea: this is what sail training teaches cadets and trainees.

After the quiet race from Norfolk, the fleet and the Class A ships arrived in Boston, where a Parade of Sail led the ships into the naval docks. Their arrival was timed to coincide with the celebrations for Boston's 250th anniversary. The ships and their crews were overwhelmed by crowds afloat and ashore. A state of emergency had to be declared as the city jammed up with traffic, despite the efforts of police and uniformed guards to bring order among the chaos.

The docks where the ships lay were opened to the public for part of each day, leaving the crews and cadets marooned on board by the sheer press of onlookers. Literally millions of people visited the port of Boston during the

The Danish three-masted staysail schooner, *Creole*, setting a genoa *(D. J. Benstead)*

Her Majesty's Sail Training Yacht, *Sabre*, photographed at the start of the Tall Ships Race from Tenerife to Bermuda, 1976

The Norwegian full-rigged training ship, *Christian Radich*, in Oslo, 1978, after the parade of tall ships from Horten when the author joined her as an AB and Captain Kjell Thorsen RNN was in command. This ship was built in 1937 and is owned by the Østlandets Skoleskibs at Oslo.

festivities of 1980. There was a feeling, though, that this degree of commercialisation was excessive since it was in danger of overshadowing the real value of the event.

The shore activities were run by 'Operation Sail', commonly known as Opsail, a completely separate entity from the American Sail Training Association which is affiliated to the Sail Training Association.

At Boston the fleet was joined by entrants for the race to Kristiansand, including the full-rigged ships *Christian Radich* from Norway and *Danmark* from Denmark, and the West German naval barque *Gorch Fock II* in Class A. Smaller vessels included the bermudan ketch *Astral*, sailed by cadets from the United States Naval Academy at Annapolis, and *Christian Venturer*, a schooner from Bermuda which is rigged with a chinese lug and owned and sailed by Robert R. Doe. There was also *El Pirata*, owned by John Cluett of Guernsey, and *Zenobe Gramme* of the Belgian Navy.

The United States Coast Guard barque *Eagle* was present at the start, but her training programme sadly confined her to home waters. The US Coast Guard laws with their complex regulations restrict the participation of many vessels in sail training.

The competitors were soon busy preparing to cross the Atlantic, taking on fuel, water and stores. *Christian Radich* had already spent a few days in dry-dock. She had voyaged from California, where her crew had joined in January; the cadets taking a preliminary six-month course on board, sailing through the Panama Canal and across the Caribbean Sea to the Gulf of Mexico, New Orleans and other ports en route to the east coast of the United States, before arriving in Boston in time for the race.

The day of the start, 4 June, was almost windless, causing a delay of two hours before the ships could set off. The vessels made their way out accompanied by thousands of small craft. The only directions were that Sable Island, lying to the south-east of Nova Scotia, and a notorious hazard to navigation, should be left to port, and that the North Ronaldsay Light, on the Orkney Islands, should remain to starboard.

Initially, it was a drifting match with the square-riggers barely moving in the sunshine, but gradually the wind rose and the ships made way, disappearing across the Atlantic horizon, to sail the 3,096 nautical miles of ocean on a fair route for Kristiansand South in Norway. Conditions ranged from the initial calm to the thick blanket of fog of the Banks of Labrador, and later to gale and storm force winds reaching over 60 knots which blew some competitors off course.

The full-rigged ship *Danmark* had to run off from the wind under her fore lower topsail, careering at 10 knots down waves 12–18 metres (40–60 feet) high. Safety lines and netting were rigged all round the decks which were lashed by the sea. On one occasion, when ten boys and a quartermaster were trying to haul in the main sheet they were lifted bodily off the deck and thrown into the scuppers. Crews were often knee-deep, even waist-deep, in the heavy seas. The mess deck was always wet, and clothing and bedding got damp with no hope of drying them. Lashed on with safety harnesses, four cadets at a time took the wheel. Look-outs stood on the boat deck rather than on the exposed fo'c'sle. The main deck was closed as a thoroughfare. The wind at hurricane Force 12 howled in the rigging, and a rough encounter with one sea damaged the port bridge wing, a solid wooden structure, and also carried the port after lifeboat away from its davits. Fortunately, this was resecured but only after hours of work in raging conditions. These storm force winds drove *Danmark* off her course and, when the weather eased, her Captain, Wilhelm Hansen, decided to retire and take the southern route up the English Channel.

Meanwhile, *Sabre* was bowling along but when the storm struck she was forced to heave to for eighteen hours. Before this she had been passed by *Creole*, 'sailing magnificently'. This classic three-masted staysail schooner built as a private yacht in 1927 by Camper and Nicholson, was a rare sight: with her sleek lines she moved through the water like the traditional ocean greyhound.

CREOLE
When the conditions eased, *Creole*'s crew were sitting on deck mending sails. An officer then decided that it was time for a cup of coffee. Not all the trainees wanted to go below, even to get out of the damp chill; but it might have been a

guardian angel who gave the order, for only seconds later the mizzen mast crashed down on to the deck near where they had been sitting. Rigging lay around everywhere and the mast, which had snapped 4 metres (13 feet) above the deck, was draped over the side of the hull. It had bent, without warning, like a banana, and fallen, thanks to the coffee break, without injuring anyone.

The students on board, who mainly came from broken or otherwise unhappy homes with problems, worked together admirably; not a grumble was heard as the wreckage was cleared under difficult conditions. For sixteen to eighteen hours the work of salving rigging and mast went on non-stop. Much of the rigging at least could be saved and used for the new mast when it was fitted at the Spencer Thetis Wharf in Cowes. And thanks to the initiative of John Hamilton and the co-operation of Harry Spencer, the replacement was ready before the ship arrived in the Isle of Wight, enabling her to sail in the first Cutty Sark Tall Ships Race of 1980. She arrived just before the start off the Danish island of Falster. Good team-work all round had paid off!

Creole's rigging continued to cause problems, however, and she was unable to carry full sail during the races. Nevertheless, she did compete, and she was *there*, which is the real meaning of these events.

There is much more to tell about the 699 tons TM Creole. She was launched in 1927 as *Vira*, and in the mid-1950s was bought by the Greek shipping magnate Stavros Niarchos. He loaned her so that British cadets could enter the first Tall Ships Race in 1956, and eventually based her in the Mediterranean, where she lay idle until the late seventies.

At that time a group of young Danish teachers from the Nyborg Søfartsskole and affiliated schools were looking for a ship so that they could take young people, especially those in need of special care and help, into a new environment where they could learn to live in society without destroying it or themselves. In the course of their search they found *Creole* lying in Piraeus in a state of disrepair. With the aid of a loan, they collected $200,000 which they sent to her owner in Greece accompanied by a letter stating that if the money was not returned by a certain date they would assume that the offer had been accepted, and would come to take delivery of the ship. As they had no reply, they went to Greece and completed the transaction. They sailed *Creole* to Denmark in 1978, although her rigging was in poor shape and the sail wardrobe was deficient. She was then re-fitted for her current training programme of six-month courses entailing long voyages across the Atlantic, when she calls at many ports and countries where the students are introduced to new ways of life ashore. Lessons are held throughout the passages to educate the youngsters in various subjects to help them to qualify for jobs on their return home. The officers and teachers themselves comply with the ship's rule—no alcohol on board—and strongly recommend the same abstinence ashore.

A new mizzen mast for *Creole* at the Spencer Thetis Wharf, Cowes, where it was replaced in time for her to compete in the Cutty Sark Tall Ships Races in Europe. Later in the year her fore and main masts were replaced at the same yard *(Patrick Eden)*

THE RESULTS

Meanwhile, the other competitors raced ahead in record time. *Blanca Estela* finished first overall and in her class with an elapsed time of just over 17 days $7\frac{1}{2}$ hours. Just over $1\frac{1}{2}$ hours later, *Gorch Fock* crossed the line, followed less than 2 hours later by *Christian Radich* who won the prize for Class A on corrected time. After a few days in Kristiansand, she returned to Oslo, her home port, where she had not tied up for nearly a year. The crew went on leave and maintenance work began at a shipyard. So she was unable to join the fleet at the Cutty Sark Tall Ships Races and, as a regular competitor, she was greatly missed.

Chaser and *Guayas* arrived two days later, while *Sabre* reported that the wind had eased up across the North Sea, and, although she did not slow down to pick up the fish offered her by some friendly fishermen, only crossed the line two days after that. The remaining entrants followed the day after, *Christian Venturer* gaining first prize in Class B on corrected time.

IN SCANDINAVIA: *GUAYAS*

Alongside in Kristiansand Harbour lay *Guayas*, the floating naval ambassador from Ecuador. This barque of 1,153 tons gross was launched in 1977 at the yard of Talleres Celaya in Spain and is a sister ship to *Gloria* of Colombia and *Simon Bolivar* of Venezuela. She carries junior officers and midshipmen from the Naval Superior School at Guayaquil on the River Guayas from which she took her name. The school was founded in 1822 by Simon Bolivar, the South American liberator who won the country its independence and created its own navy, formed mainly by experienced foreign seamen. Two Englishmen, Admiral Juan Illingworth (could this be a forebear of the great racing yachtsman and designer who played an important part in the initial organisation of these Tall Ships Races?) and Thomas Wright Montgomery, along with an American, Joseph Villamil from Louisiana, helped to establish this new navy which, since these early days, has expanded and was recently modernised. Now, it has adopted sail training for the cadets. Captain Nelson Armas told me that his country is convinced that in an age of electronics and mechanical devices this is still the best way for sailors to learn seamanship and to live and work together.

Ecuador has been described as a country 'small, rich and majestic'. Rich in variety, it ranges from the terrain of the high Andes to the Amazonian jungle on one side, the narrow coastal plain on the Pacific, equatorial rain forest in the south, and 656 miles out in the Pacific Ocean, the unique islands of Galapagos, abundant with extraordinary flora and fauna. It is also a country steeped in history and culture, delving back to the pre-Colombian era, which was succeeded later by the Incas. A few precious relics of that age were exhibited on board *Guayas*.

LINDØ

It was morning and the band was playing as I watched the officers and sailors, smartly turned out in white uniforms. Near by lay the three-masted topsail schooner *Lindo*. Chrissie, the wife of the Master, Greg Walker, invited me to

Ecuadorian barque *Guayas*, launched in 1977, seen here at Kristiansand, her bowsprit rising high above the cars on the quayside

visit them and, when I was aboard, I talked to some of the crew who had raced across the Atlantic, including Bill, the silver-haired Australian Mate—a real seafaring character. This was his first trip to Europe after years spent roaming the Pacific and Caribbean under sail. I then talked to the Skipper in his cabin with its traditional homely atmosphere, enhanced by the plants which he had bought on a recent shopping expedition, replacements for the worst damage suffered during the Atlantic storm!

Chilean naval yacht, the Swan 65 *Blanca Estela*, leaving Kristiansand

Greg Walker talked to me about the preparations that had had to be made over the previous two years for the transatlantic voyage. The normal charter routine in the Caribbean and east coast of the United States went on while the rigging was being completely overhauled, the spars checked and revarnished from bare wood, and sails, hull—everything, in fact—maintained to keep the high standards which were conspicuously evident above and below decks.

Lindø was built in Sweden in 1928, and sailed from Scandinavia to the West Indies and Newfoundland as a cargo ship trading in rum, molasses, salt, fish and hardware. In 1973 her bare hull was found by two Danes and an American who immediately set to work to make her seaworthy again. Three years later she appeared at the Millbay Docks in Plymouth, ready to take part in the STA Races to the USA. After the race, she was noticed by two young American vets who followed her back to Europe, made the owners an offer, and soon a splendid ship was theirs, re-registered in Delaware and run by a skipper and permanent crew of eight. For the ASTA Race she carried trainees at a cost well below the normal charter fee and she was placed second in her class on corrected time for the 1980 race from Boston to Kristiansand.

BLANCA ESTELA AND *CHRISTIAN VENTURER*

On a quay opposite *Guayas* lay the Chilean Naval Swan 65, *Blanca Estela*. In command was Captain John Martin, a retired naval officer who gained the affection as well as the respect of his crew. His skilful seamanship was tested in 1976 aboard the Chilean naval four-masted barquentine *Esmeralda*, sister ship to the Spanish *Juan Sebastian de Elcano*. Aboard her he competed in the STA Race from Bermuda to Newport, and has become a familiar member of the training world, easily distinguished by his charming smile and the vice-like hook of his artificial arm which is adjustable to cope with almost anything, even a wine glass.

Alongside lay *Christian Venturer*. She was built in Bermuda by her owner/ Skipper Bob Doe for fishing and some charter work. Her rig is unusual, combining a schooner lug with junk sails, which apparently can be braced well round and proves successful. The hull is long and narrow with a steering position aft below, completely sheltered and protected in rough weather. On the mizzen mast there is a wind vane for providing power to charge the batteries. Bob Doe sailed her with five trainees and two mates, one of whom, Bob Wallis, had had a career at sea sailing around the world on the brigantine *Romance* and cruising on the schooner *The Pride of Baltimore*.

KRISTIANSAND SOUTH

The morning of 3 July was bright and clear as I went to meet Colonel Dick Scholfield, the previous Race Director of the STA who was acting as technical adviser and calculator expert for the ASTA Race across the Atlantic. He told me that the race had been exceptionally fast, breaking all previous averages for past Tall Ships Races. *Blanca Estela* averaged 179 miles a day; *Gorch Fock*, 178 miles a day; *Christian Radich*, 177 miles a day (a speed of 7.4 knots); *Guayas*, 158 miles a day; *Lindø*, 140 miles a day, and *Christian Venturer*, 136 miles a day.

These exceptional speeds brought the ships in far earlier than expected, although the weather had forced others to retire. Radio contact was not always maintained between the ships. *El Pirata*, for one, was only spotted in mid-Atlantic by the liner *QE2* and, having retired, was next heard of via a telephone message from Scotland! This was not a navigational 'nasty' but sensible routing through the Caledonian Canal, as she had been driven south during the storm and needed to reach East Anglia in time to pick up a crew from Mariners International for the Cutty Sark Tall Ships Races in Europe.

Zenobe Gramme, the Belgian Navy ketch, had been forced to retire early in the race, a few hundred miles from the start, when her forestay parted. She returned to Halifax, Nova Scotia, for repairs.

Not all the participants that finished could afford to wait for the organised programme in Kristiansand. *Astral*, for example, a large white bermudan ketch, generously given by Cornelius Vanderstar to the United States Naval Academy, had raced across the Atlantic but had to go on to represent her country at Aalborg in Denmark where the largest Independence Day celebrations outside the USA take place annually at the Rebild Festival, near the city. Crewed by eighteen cadets, this naval training yacht had an interesting race, and, when the steering broke down, their resourcefulness was tested. In the later stages she relied on an auto-pilot which was still functioning and took a time penalty as a result. It is one of the conditions of these sail-training races that the trainees and cadets must steer—no modern self-steering devices, or automatic helms are allowed. At Aalborg *Astral* happily met *Danmark* after she had arrived by the southern route.

Thus the fleet had dwindled by the time the official programme was due to begin. The early arrivals were welcomed with lavish hospitality, although it was a great disappointment to the city that most of the official programme, including the visit of King Olaf of Norway, had to be cancelled—particularly as he is a great enthusiast for sail training. (In 1978 he presented the prizes in Oslo after the races, and Lieutenant-Commander, the Honourable Greville Howard, against the usual royal protocol, called three cheers for King Olaf, which he himself echoed the following year at the Manx Millennium Sail Training Rally.) The city of Kristiansand nevertheless organised numerous sporting events and social occasions and there was much private entertaining. Although King Olaf was not present the Royal Military Band and Guard did the honours to perfection.

Kristiansand was founded in 1641 by King Christian IV, King of Denmark and Norway, on a sandy spit at the mouth of the River Otra—hence 'Christian's sand'. Its founder was a keen architect and town planner who laid out the streets on a regular chequerboard pattern, as can be seen on a map of the city as it stands today. The main part of this original complex lies surrounded on two sides by the sea and by the River Otra with the hills rising away to the north-west on the landward side.

Local farmers were forced to come into the city to create the initial population. Many of the houses were built around courtyards with barn-type doors and housing for livestock. The older, traditional buildings lie at the northern part of the city. Flowers abound in the gardens and on the walls of the houses in

Norwegian prawn picnic: Ecuadorian sailors on a boat trip to Lillesand

summertime. The cathedral in the market square dominates the scene. The sea can be glimpsed in various places from the streets, glistening on the island-studded coastline which is ideal for summer expeditions and day cruising.

The first Sunday was peaceful, with time to relax and explore the island route eastwards from Kristiansand to Lillesand. The neatly white-painted wooden houses which nestle among the creeks and winding passageways are mostly holiday homes. Some of the officers and cadets of *Guayas* were treated to a typical Norwegian prawn feast in this wonderful scenery—just one example of the local hospitality. Inland lie the lakes and mountains of the region of Sørlandet. The city has expanded beyond its original bounds and now has a population of about 60,000.

One evening there was a party for the competitors of the ASTA Race and *Sørlandet* at the Caledonian Hotel, with a drama competition between the ships' crews. The cadets' performances on stage had to be intelligible to all the nationalities present. The *Sørlandet* contingent sang a shanty and the *Blanca Estela* boys performed a mime of a young man being harassed by an insistent mosquito to such effect that the audience almost felt threatened. The company from *Guayas* performed an operation on an agonised patient who was hauled on to a table by his white-coated companions to have the offending organ removed with wire-cutters and rigging tools!

The crew of *Lindø* then re-enacted in mime their passage from the USA, and the voyage to Boston from the West Indies. Sunshine was portrayed by palm trees, bikinis, sun-glasses and tropical music. The crew were lying completely relaxed inside a vast cardboard model of their ship. The scenery, which filled the stage, was bedecked with a dinghy mast and sail. An Atlantic storm was simulated by a cadet throwing buckets of water across the stage, while loud, crashing music emphasised the force of the gale. The change to *piano* indicated the calm that preceded the ship's arrival at Kristiansand and champagne bottles popped to mark the award of second prize in their class. Their prize for their performance on this occasion was a first!

Without the spoken word, a group of international youngsters had entertained each other, communicating through the common language of mime and song. The evening was a great success.

The festivities in Kristiansand were now drawing to a close and preparations had to be made prior to setting sail. Refuelled, re-stored, revictualled and repairs completed, the ships were soon en route to ports further south, heading for Kiel.

2

KRISTIANSAND TO KIEL ABOARD *SØRLANDET*

I shall slip on board by boat or along hawser; and then one morning I shall wake to the song and tramp of the sailors, the clink of the capstan, and the rattle of the anchor-chain coming merrily in. We shall break out the jib and the foresail, the white houses on the harbour side will glide slowly past us as she gathers steering-way, and the voyage will have begun! As she forges towards the headland she will clothe herself with canvas; and then, once outside, the sounding slap of great green seas as she heels to the wind, pointing South!

KENNETH GRAHAME, *The Wind in the Willows*

Until I arrived in Kristiansand I had not fully realised the work involved to recommission a square-rigger safely and efficiently, but I soon appreciated what an achievement it was on *Sørlandet*.

The full-rigged ship was built in 1927 by P. Høivolds Mek Verksted at Kristiansand. Named after the southern region of Norway which means 'south land', she is 644 tons TM, 568 tons gross, and measures 57 metres (186 feet) length overall. She was ordered as a training ship for the Norwegian Merchant Navy to be run by the Sørlandets Seilende Skoleskibs Institution, financed by a legacy provided by the ship-owner O. A. T. Skjelbred, who had died in 1918.

Her career began in northern Europe but she was soon making transatlantic passages. At the outbreak of war in 1939 she was taken over by the Royal Norwegian Navy and stationed at Horten Naval Base where she was later captured by the Germans who took her north to the port of Kirkenes on the USSR frontier. She was sunk there during a Russian attack on the Germans and lay submerged in the harbour area until she was refloated and towed south to her home port, where she served as a German submarine depot ship. In 1948, after three years of restoration work, she set sail again. The Chief Mate in 1980, Tor Kvanvig, was a cadet on board for that cruise and had subsequently served on board the *Christian Radich* for twelve years and participated in a number of Tall Ships Races.

In 1972 the Sørlandets Institution sold the ship and replaced her with a motor vessel. The ship-owner Jan Staubo bought *Sørlandet* and kept her at the nearby harbour of Tvedestrand until 1977, when his company was in financial difficulties, and she was put up for sale by auction. The descendants of the original benefactor, Skjelbreds Rederi A/S, bought her back again and donated her to the city of Kristiansand. Since then she has undergone a thorough refit, with the help of voluntary labour by private people.

Looking aloft aboard *Sørlandet*: the main royal already secured, while the main topgallant is in the process of being bunted and clewed up. Once this is completed the cadets can lay aloft to furl the sails

The Norwegian full-rigged ship, *Sørlandet*, under full sail again after seven years of idleness *(Kjell M. Olsen)*

All sail stowed: final work aloft
on *Sørlandet*

A Board of Directors was established to run the ship under the chairmanship of the Mayor, Paul Otto Johnsen, and a member of the Skjelbreds family and other distinguished citizens. The day the ship returned to the city a group of local enthusiasts formed a supporting organisation called the Friends of *Sørlandet*, of which the County Governor of Vest-Agder, Bue Fjermeros, is the Patron and Chairman, and Halfdan Tangen is Vice-Chairman. The aim is to recruit members worldwide to publicise the ship and her activities and to help financially. They have encouraged companies to purchase new gear; for instance, sails were bought and in this way a complete new set was made in Hong Kong.

A Project Manager, Commander Kongevold, took charge of the administration from the shore office. He keeps in close touch with the ship, and his secretary, Signe Klepp, acted as radio operator in the 1980 races.

Arne Fosseli was elected by the Board of Friends in January 1979 to direct the restoration. He is the retired manager of the local shipyard, and he personally gave over 4,000 hours of work and recruited bands of helpers from school children and housewives to pensioners and skilled craftsmen. All their enthusiasm and skills were ploughed into the scheme because they wanted to see the ship sail again.

All was done to meet the highest standards: safety equipment was renewed, automatic sprinklers and smoke sniffers fitted, and fire extinguishers, fire-fighting suits, life-jackets, lifeboats and harnesses bought as well as the latest aids to navigation. Nearly everything was renewed: engines, propeller shaft, generators, freezers, and all lighting and wiring. The galley was completely re-equipped with new cookers and all modern machines including a dish-washer. All bedding and upholstery were replaced, as were the miles of ropes and running rigging. Every detail mattered, every shackle pin was important, and it was all the responsibility of the Captain, Nils Arntsen, who first sailed on *Sørlandet* as a cadet in 1932 for five months. The ship was then five years old and carried ninety cadets. He left to join the four-masted barque *Hussar*, now called *Sea Cloud*, as an ordinary seaman to sail to Miami and the Pacific. Later, he signed on as Quartermaster on *Sørlandet* and, in between attending shore courses at navigational and radio schools, he remained with the ship until the outbreak of war. In the fifties he returned as Chief Officer, and was first appointed as Master in 1964. After the ship was sold in 1972 by the Sørlandets Institution he remained as head of the shore school until 1980, when he took charge of her again.

There are now sixteen qualified crew including Chief Mate, Tor Kvanvig, a First and Second Mate, chief engineer, radio operators, steward, cook, and the Bosun, Ben, who had worked on *Christian Radich* and *Svanen*, a three-masted gaff schooner owned by the Norwegian Maritime Museum at Oslo, and on which Anne, an ordinary seaman, and Helge, the Sergeant, had also worked. The sail-maker was Michael Schollin, a well-trained Swedish seaman, who began his nautical career on the Danish full-rigged ship *Georg Stage*, which he rejoined as a quartermaster and then later sailed aboard *Christian Radich* as an AB for some years, and gained further experience on other vessels.

The mess deck had been carefully refitted with bunks instead of the traditional

Making fast aboard *Sørlandet*: cadet Martin Smith, Master Mariner, one of the experienced sailors who joined her from Mariners International

Cadets on *Sørlandet* furling sail on royal and topgallant yards

hammocks, in an imaginative and practical way to accommodate seventy boy and girl trainees. During the races she carried an average of twenty female trainees, who performed all the normal duties of scrubbing decks, heaving on halliards and climbing the rigging. The last is a nerve-tingling experience on the first ascent, especially where the futtock shrouds present an awkward obstacle which can only be surmounted by using all the strength in your arms and determination, particularly at the point where legs disappear at an outrageous angle beneath you before you gain the top of the platform. Butterflies flutter in the stomach and knees feel like jelly, but the girls climbed quite as well as the boys and the manoeuvre became less frightening with familiarity.

Some of the Norwegian boys, like Erik Liebermann and his brother Geir, Erik Arntsen, son of the Captain, and the girls, Tove Merete Lande and Kjersti Moe, had helped throughout the past eighteen months on board the ship, and were a valuable asset at sea in helping the new trainees to find their way around and to know the ship and her ways generally. The new band of cadets arrived with no time for a shakedown cruise and few had any idea of sailing square-riggers; the group of ten who had come through Mariners International were the exceptions, however.

One of the crew, Steve Glenn, was working as a rigger on board, having arrived some months earlier to help in the preparations. He had already sailed around the world on the *Eye of the Wind*. Another experienced mariner was Captain Martin Smith, who had skippered the Mariners International entry *Phoenix*, the smallest Class A competitor in the 1976 Tall Ships Race, but this time he was sailing as a trainee in order to learn more about square-rig, possibly with an eye to the future of commercial sail. Another qualified hand was Lieutenant Frank Scott, RN, who had sailed aboard *Sørlandet* as a cadet in 1968 on a voyage which included the 1968 Tall Ships Race from Gothenburg to Kristiansand via an oil rig, and who was in command of *Marques* entered by Mariners International in the 1978 race from Great Yarmouth to Oslo.

The others were not quite so experienced, and thirty-five of them had flown from Boston for the race as far as Karlskrona, where *Sørlandet* would change crews.

The cadets varied as much in nationality as in occupation. There were students, secretaries, engineers, a dentist, a boatyard mechanic, a chauffeur and a carpenter. Two of the boys came from Sweden with the help of the Abraham Rydberg Foundation which for many years has trained cadets for the Swedish Merchant Navy.

Now *Sørlandet* was setting sail, after shore drills hastily carried out in a few hours instead of the usual weeks on a square-rigger. The eyes of the city were upon us as we hoisted sail in the bay. The wind was not in our favour and we had to beat against an easterly which sent us down to the coast of Denmark, near the Hanstholm Light, about 90 degrees off our desired track, and on the next tack we managed only to return to our original departure point! However, when another tack took us back to the coast of Denmark, with little progress, the decision was taken to motor up to the northern headland of Skagen on the Danish coast where we could set a fair course towards Kiel. The trainees were getting a good initiation into life at sea, working a two-watch system and coming to know the sails and rigging. Particular enthusiasts could often be seen clutching notebooks and diagrams while examining the cordage and numerous belaying pins on deck.

There was one 'youngster' aboard who had learnt the ropes in the days of trading sail, and had even been shipwrecked on the *Garthpool*, the last British trading square-rigger. Stan Hugill, a well-known authority on shanties, climbed up the rigging with ease, outwardly denying any sign of his seventy-four years. His role was mainly before the BBC television camera on board which was recording the passage to Kiel for a programme in *The World About Us* series, produced by Tony Salmon with the assistance of Simon Normanton. Naturally, Stan always had a seafaring yarn or two, and a shanty with which to fill an idle moment.

MARINERS INTERNATIONAL

Mariners International, an organisation based in London, is in its own words: 'A non-profit association devoted to the preservation and promotion of traditional sailing vessels and of the arts, skills and lore that are related to them.' It was created in 1974 to provide berths for enthusiasts in the Tall Ships Race that year,

Stan Hugill, shantyman, on *Sørlandet* during engine trials off Kristiansand South

for which the group chartered a vessel. Since then, Mariners has entered various traditional sailing vessels in the races, notably the brigantine *Phoenix* in 1976, whose voyage was described by Jenni Atkinson, then Secretary of Mariners, in *A Girl in Square-Rig,* later entitled *A Girl Before the Mast.*

In 1978, for the Tall Ships Race from Great Yarmouth to Oslo, they sailed *Marques,* a barque more commonly known as the *Beagle* for her part in the television series on Darwin. In 1980, as well as filling *El Pirata,* Mariners also organised ten berths for members aboard *Sørlandet.*

Activities are not restricted to the Tall Ships Races. Cruises are organised on topsail schooners, Baltic traders, Thames barges and various sailing ships. Emphasis is placed on the promotion and preservation of traditional craft, and the maintenance of the skills of seamanship. Maritime history, archaeology and the protection of the sea environment are all given special attention. Their shoreside social functions held occasionally each year, usually in London, prove very popular. They include shows of rare maritime films and nautical discussions.

Members of Mariners must be at least fifteen years of age, but apart from that, they are not restricted by geography or expertise. The organisation is run entirely by volunteers, and produces a quarterly newsletter *Notices to Mariners International,* packed with details about vessels. The Chairman and Editor is Erik Abranson, an expert enthusiast on traditional sail and an author who is also a trustee of the World Ship Trust.

Sunset: *Sørlandet* silhouette

The crew of *Donald Searle*, the London Sailing Project bermudan ketch, commissioned in 1980. These officers and trainees participated in Race One and the cruise-in-company, leaving the ship at Frederikshavn where a new crew joined for Race Two *(D. J. Benstead)*

3

ARRIVAL AT KIEL

I cannot tell their wonder nor make known
Magic that once thrilled me to the bone,
But all men praise some beauty, tell some tale,
Vent a high mood which makes the rest seem pale.

JOHN MASEFIELD, 'Ships'

We anchored in the Kiel Fiord on Saturday 12 July to be ready for entering the city on the following morning. We eagerly awaited the arrival of our fellow competitors, and during the day the British Sea Cadet Corps brig TS *Royalist* anchored near by us. Built in 1971, to the designs of Colin Mudie in association with Lieutenant-Commander Morin Scott, RNR, she was inspired by the success of the brigantine *Centurion*, which, on loan to the Sea Cadet Corps, had won the Tall Ships Race from Falmouth to Copenhagen in 1966. HMS *Falken* from Sweden lay close by.

That afternoon, while all day yachts and spectator craft circled the fiord, there was some fine sailing by yachts belonging to the British Kiel Yacht Club, including three which would be participating in the race—*Avalanche, Flamingo* and *Kranich*—all of them with classic pre-war lines under full sail. Quite spontaneously, I complimented *Kranich*, which passed close by our stern, with, 'You do look lovely!' Later, I discovered that the skipper, Lieutenant-Colonel Roger Cemm, was uncertain whether to take this remark personally or not as he felt it was addressed to the man in charge! This caused some amusement when we met as I was unaware of the identity of the crew whom I had so addressed, and he greeted me with, 'You're the girl who said I looked lovely, or was it my boat?'

These 100-square metre windfall yachts are the remainder of those which became the basis of the British Kiel Yacht Club after World War II when a group of sapper officers gathered up all the available prize yachts from the Baltic area. These included 30-, 50-, 75- and 100-square metre yachts, gracefully designed with wooden hulls and tall masts. The sappers were helped by the pre-war Olympic yachtsman, Herr Bruno Splieth, to retrieve these scattered prizes, and he has remained with the club ever since, acting as its Harbour Master. During the race from Falster to Karlskrona *Flamingo* was skippered by Major-General J. P. Groom, CBE, then Commodore of the British Kiel Yacht Club, and *Avalanche* was under the command of Major M. W. B. Best, RE, the Commandant of the Kiel Training Centre.

The club is run by a committee of representatives chosen from its members of the British Army serving in West Germany. It organises numerous sail-training courses from Kiel, sailing around the Danish islands and Baltic coast. In 1980 there were enough berths to accommodate 3,500 trainees for one week each in that season. In order to qualify for government aid, 75 per cent of the sea-time of these club-owned boats must be devoted to giving soldiers sail training. The rest of the fleet includes Contessa 32s and 28s and Rebels. The Army regards this activity as an important part of general training for teaching the young men and women to confront fear, realise strength of character and gain a sense of responsibility and leadership. So courses, which include the RYA/DTI Certificate Scheme, are run throughout the summer at this large club and some vessels are available on charter to members. The gleaming varnish and smart paintwork of these 100-square metre entrants in the Cutty Sark International Tall Ships Race confirmed their high standard of maintenance.

Later, the London Sailing Project's new vessel *Donald Searle* sailed close by under our stern. Launched in 1979, this standard Tyler moulded van der Stadt hull was fitted out to the designs of Tony Sharples, a naval architect who understood exactly what was needed. She was completed at Southern Ocean Shipyard. Every detail of her layout was carefully planned: fire and safety equipment, electrics, cabling, tanks, an accessible engine-room below the cockpit, rigging, bunks and crew space.

The LSP developed initially because Lord Amory, then Minister of Agriculture and Fisheries, met Lieutenant-Commander Walter Scott, OBE, DSC, RN, at the Westminster Sea Scout unit which he ran. The Minister asked if some of the boys could help take his 14-metre (48-foot) LOA yacht *Ailanthus* along the coast, and so it was arranged that youngsters from London boys' clubs and the Sea Scout movement went to sea. The bermudan ketch *Rona* was bought through the generosity of Lord Amory himself. He continued to finance all the costs of running the project until recent years when, owing to inflation, additional financial aid was necessary.

Walter Scott was a leading light in the original concept, which still runs in the manner of the intrepid bumble-bee, for if it ever stopped to calculate how it flew it would find that theory made it impossible. Thus, the project runs from day to day fired by the endless supply of enthusiasm which all its skippers and officers, who have often been trainees themselves, generate.

Based at Gosport, there were three vessels in 1980—*Rona, Gunna* and *Donald Searle*—which are run by a staff of two who take care of maintenance and changeovers. Johnny Griffiths has been in charge since 1973, and has ship-hand Tom Reynolds to help him.

The LSP has only missed one Tall Ships Race since 1962 and in 1976 chartered *GBII* from Chay Blyth, with the help of Woolworth's and other sponsors, for the transatlantic series to the USA and back. The emblem of the project is a weaver bird, supporter of Lord Amory's crest.

All the boys who attend the courses come from London boys' clubs, the Sea Cadets and Sea Scouts. They are usually a mixed bunch as it is more beneficial to run the courses with boys who do not all know each other. The berths are subsidised so that the cost in 1980, including transport from London and back, was £15. The low cost enables as many youngsters as possible to join the boats for either a week in the summer or three weekends in spring or autumn. Those trainees who show seamanship and leadership potential may be asked to return as watch leaders and even later may progress up the scale, gaining the appropriate RYA/DTI Certificates en route, in order to skipper the boats. Many sail-training enthusiasts, including Lieutenant-Colonel James Myatt, Captain Chris Phelan, David Cobb, John Hamilton, and Ian Fisher, sail with the London Sailing Project.

SHIP-SHAPE AND NORWEGIAN FASHION!

During the day work continued aboard *Sørlandet*. She was a hive of activity for we aimed to create an especially good impression as all eyes would be on this ship which had disappeared from the sailing scene for over seven years. Some of the trainees worked aloft and on deck while others were detailed below to wash and scrub the mess and officers' quarters. Some of us found a dust-sucker and attacked the cushions and seats of the bunks. It was some hours before all was ship-shape and we could relax for the evening.

It was peaceful on deck, watching the passing water traffic. Below, gentle conversation filled the air, for by now many of the crew had become acquainted. Anchor watches were maintained and regular safety checks were made above and below decks. In harbour, a small watch party of eight to ten trainees under an officer was on duty at all times.

At 0630 the duty officer swept through the mess deck calling all hands. By 0700 the chores were well under way. Soon, everything shone from the brass binnacle to the ship's bell, from the chef's hat to the 'heads' and wash-rooms (the latter two I can guarantee, having scrubbed and polished them vigorously myself). The ship was now ready.

KRUZENSHTERN

During breakfast our rivals began to make their way up to the quays, and, when the word went round that *Kruzenshtern* was passing by, the mess deck emptied, breakfast lost its appeal and the decks were lined with clicking cameras. The Russian four-masted barque's size is impressive: she is 3,185 Thames tons, 3,064 registered tons and 114.5 metres (376 feet) length overall, has a beam of 14 metres (46 feet), a mainmast height of 56 metres ($183\frac{1}{2}$ feet) above the waterline, 52 metres ($170\frac{1}{2}$ feet) above deck, and a sail area of 3,656 square metres. Built in 1926 as the *Padua* by the yard of Tecklenborg at Bremerhaven, West Germany, for the famous Laeisz Flying 'P' Line, she originally carried cargoes of nitrates from Chile, and later wool from Australia. After World War II she was taken over by the USSR as a training vessel, and since the sixties has been refitted completely for use by the Russian Fisheries Service. She sails for ten months of the year with cadets on board.

Her distinctive black and white hull accentuates her huge proportions. Little

Russian cadets manning the yards of the four-masted barque, *Kruzenshtern*, at Bremerhaven, West Germany, 1980 *(Stadtbildstelle Seestadt Bremerhaven)*

did I imagine that later on during the races I should have the opportunity of fulfilling a great dream by sailing on board her, even to steer her, and climb aloft on those high masts!

SEA CLOUD

In contrast, although of similar rig and size, *Sea Cloud*, 2,700 Thames tons, 107.5 metres (353 feet) length overall, and with a sail area of 3,160 square metres, passed by in the opposite direction, heading out to sea for a day charter. I say in contrast, because this ship was built as a wedding present from E. F. Hutton to his millionairess bride Marjorie in 1931, at a cost of $900,000, and she is as luxurious as ever today.

Sailing along with the races, she accompanied the fleet, although she could not actually participate owing to her crew ratio. The STA Race Rules specify that 50 per cent of the total complement on board a vessel must be as follows: the age range for Class B ships is 16 to 25 inclusive for cadets and trainees and for Class A 15-year-olds are allowed making the range 15 to 25 inclusive—*Sea Cloud* was only carrying twenty trainees.

Nearly fifty years before the 1980 races, *Sea Cloud* was launched as *Hussar* in Kiel, at the Germania Shipyard. She has undergone many changes of name in her history: *Hussar*, then *Sea Cloud, Angelita, Patria* and latterly *Antarna*. She was originally painted black in keeping with all the vessels which E. F. Hutton had previously owned and called *Hussar*, but this new one was the greatest, out-classing her predecessors. He made long voyages with her each year to harbours all round the world.

When Marjorie Hutton divorced her husband, she kept the *Hussar* but changed her name to *Sea Cloud* and had her hull painted white. In 1937 her new husband Joseph Davies was appointed American Ambassador to the Soviet Union, and he took *Sea Cloud* with him.

During World War II she was placed at the disposal of the United States Coast Guard who had an engine fitted to the hull and used her for hunting submarines. She was used for this purpose until 1945, by which time the comforts on board were considerably diminished.

Although in a poor state, she was refitted for cruising and, as the old gold bath taps shone again, luxury returned. Meantime, however, costs had risen and $40,000 a year were needed to clothe and pay the crew alone. So in 1954 she was sold, out of the American flag, to Señor Trujillo, Dictator of the Dominican Republic, who changed her name to *Angelita* and mounted a gun on deck. Seven years later he was assassinated and she became the property of a businessman in Louisiana who renamed her *Patria*. She was laid up eventually in Panama, under the name of *Antarna*.

She is owned now by a group of ten Hamburg businessmen, including Captain Paschburg, who has since written and compiled a book on her history, published in Germany. Refitted in Hamburg, and registered in the Grand Cayman Islands, she sails in the luxurious style for which she was built. She accommodates eighty passengers and has a crew of about sixty to look after them all and man the sails—there are fewer to look after the sails than the customers, in fact.

During the races there were about twenty youngsters from different national-ities on board who worked the ship under the guidance of the full-time crew of sailmaker, bosun and ABs.

CALL ALL HANDS!

It was time to call all hands to man the capstan and raise *Sørlandet*'s anchor and leave for Kiel. It took about an hour to bring up the massive chain, aided by our colourful shantyman, Stan Hugill, who sang a hearty version of 'South Aus-tralia'. The tune echoed across the water as the anchor rose to the tramp of the boys and girls marching around the foredeck with the capstan bars before them.

Raising anchor: cadets and trainees manning the capstan aboard *Sørlandet* in the Kiel fiord

Although Stan endeavours to maintain the words and traditions of the shanty, nowadays the fast pace on board a training ship does not comply with the rhythm of the tunes. These originally developed to encourage the work of short-handed crews and to maintain the regular impetus of effort, when strength was needed most. A good shantyman was said to be worth the weight of ten men on board, but nowadays there is no shortage of hands on training ships. Nevertheless, shantying as an international pastime thrives and is very popular, as was evident during the races.

As the BBC cameras filmed this mixture of the traditional and modern, the anchor rose to a great chorus, and we were under way towards our quayside destination.

SOMERSET

The radar-training vessel *Somerset* passed us en route. She was on loan from the Southampton College of Nautical Studies at Warsash as the HQ for the Sail Training Association and the Cutty Sark Tall Ships Race Office—the mother ship for the fleet. In command was Captain Chris Phelan, Director of the College, and a member of the STA Sailing Committee. An ebullient character, whose enthusiasm is infectious, he regards high standards and cheerfulness as essential and runs his ship accordingly. The rest of the crew comprised officers from the college, John Clark, First Officer, whose wife was also on board, and Bob Craig, the engineer.

Peggy Phelan, the Captain's wife was there, always smiling and stalwart, helping everyone. Their son Carl played an active role in the team and his

The stern of *Sørlandet*, with *Dar Pomorza* in the background, at Kiel

brother Martin competed on *Cereola*. Brian Evans of the Sailing Committee was there during the races too, and also official STA photographer D. J. Benstead.

The cadets on board came mostly from the London Sailing Project and took great pride in their ship. The efficiency and discipline on board was the backbone of the administration and communication throughout the events. *Somerset* appeared to run like clockwork (any minor hiccups were never evident). She ran as a training ship to a strict routine. In harbour, her crew rose without exception every day at 0530. Braced by cups of tea, the decks were washed and scrubbed down by the boys while below the ladies washed the shirts of the whole crew, who always appeared in uniform, with navy STA epaulettes attached to the shoulder. By 0800 all had to be ready on board as the official Race Office was open, and from then on there would be cadets on duty to deliver papers and messages to the ships. They also acted as mobile patrol units in small speed boats with walkie-talkie radio sets.

One member of the company who must not go unrecorded was Gaylen, who had joined the crew from Bermuda where she was first attracted to the tall ships in 1976. She longed to rejoin them and in the summer of 1980 was gallantly amid the culinary delights of ship board life—stores under the floors where you stand to cook, people always wishing to pass through the galley at the moment the hatch is lifted, and rolling seas when nothing stays where it is put.

Somerset was eager to arrive, as she had been delayed by one day and had to set up the Cutty Sark International Tall Ships Race Office as soon as she docked. In

Crew of *Somerset*, singing a song aboard *Danmark* for a radio programme in Karlskrona

fact, John Hamilton, Race Director, and his secretary, Mrs Jo Brigham, were waiting on the quay.

ARRIVAL QUAY

After a rush of activity, we were almost there. Masts and yards came into view; we could see bermudan rig, square-rig, gaff sails, junk sails, flags flying, and crowds on the quays.

As we neared the quay, we stood in line on deck and looked at the sailors on *Gorch Fock, Guayas* and *Kruzenshtern*, and at the hundreds of onlookers on shore. We observed many smiling faces and looked forward to making friends with some of the crews later.

I remembered Bernard Morgan whose idea to gather together young people (initially mainly boys) from different countries to participate in healthy competition inspired these races. It must have been his dream to see what he began in 1956 maturing to this international occasion in 1980.

Our ship, *Sørlandet*, attracted special attention for there were about twenty girls on board—an unusual sight on a large square-rigger and one which made history during the races—and we noticed surprised reactions among other crews as we passed.

The inexperienced crew had by now integrated well and was ready for the race. First, however, there were festivities to enjoy ashore in Kiel.

WINDJAMMERTREFFEN 80

After we had docked with the help of tugs, a Liaison Officer came on board and the Captain and Chief Officer learnt about the forthcoming programme. Everyone on board was given a badge displaying an emblem of a semaphore signaller. This would give them free entrance to the organised events and free transportation during the festivities of *Windjammertreffen 80*; as was noted in the English translation of the official programme, though, it was 'a badge to identify the wearer as a participant entitled to visit the events and to use the busses and tramps free of charge'. I hope the 'tramps' were well used!

Everyone on board the ships received a copy of the special LP record of shanties sung by the *Holtenauer Lotsenchor Knurrhahn*, the Kiel Pilots Choir—a generous memento of the few days spent in this city in northern Germany, which had previously hosted the tall ships in 1972 at the time of the Olympic Games, when they sailed in a cruise in company from Malmö in Sweden.

Kiel's history dates back to 1242, since when it has been an important place in the province of Schleswig-Holstein, and it is now one of the most modern cities in the Federal Republic of Germany, with a population in 1980 of 256,000. There is a modern university, an opera house, a fine town hall and many other notable buildings. Ship-building and machinery making are its important industries. Kiel Week is its most memorable annual event, when boats compete in the regatta on the fiord—an occasion due to celebrate its centenary in 1982.

The officials involved with the 1980 tall ships events were the Chairman of the Kiel Committee, Oberbürgermeister Günther Bantzer, the Harbour Master,

Georg Stage, full-rigged ship from Denmark, dressed overall at Kiel, with visitors
waiting to board her

The gaff schooner, *Hoshi*, owned by the Island Cruising Club of Salcombe setting sail en route out of Dartmouth, 1978

Hafenkapitän Jochen Morgenroth, and the Chief Naval Officer, Fregatten-kapitän Noack.

With much information to be gathered from the tall ships, I progressed along the quay, first calling aboard the hospitable *Guayas*, last seen in Kristiansand, and then at the Race Office on *Somerset*, which was alive with activity—fielding entrants, handing out instructions and notices, and answering queries from the predictable rush of eighty participating vessels. This onslaught was coped with admirably by John Hamilton, Jo Brigham and the STA team of voluntary enthusiasts, which included Commander Norman Sawyer, RN, and Ian Fisher, that remarkable young sailing ambassador who manages all types of problems and people. Among such activity I moved on to ease the congestion.

HOSHI

Along the quay I came across the gaff schooner *Hoshi* which belongs to the Island Cruising Club of Salcombe in South Devon. Designed by Charles E. Nicholson in 1909, she is a fine example of Camper and Nicholson's Yard which was represented during the races by the 1887 schooner *Amphitrite*, the staysail schooner *Creole*, and the modern collection of Nicholson 55s from the Joint Services Sailing Centre at Gosport—Her Majesty's Sail Training Yachts *British Soldier, Dasher* and *Sabre*.

Hoshi was launched as a graceful, spacious and comfortable cruising yacht, and initially included the refinement of a bath. After some years on the south coast she was based at Merseyside, and then the Menai Straits, whence she sailed to the Clyde and West Highlands. During the winter her gleaming white hull was maintained at a Cornish port. After various owners, she was used for chartering, and in 1951 joined *Provident*, the Brixham trawler, to form the basis of the Island Cruising Club. In 1970 she won the STA Tall Ships Race from Plymouth to La Coruña with an all-female crew of trainees and officers, under the command of Judy Russell and the Mate Verity Lyster, both of whom worked for the club for many years.

THE ISLAND CRUISING CLUB

The Island Cruising Club boats have participated in many STA Races, and in fact *Provident* competed in 1956 with Commander A. H. (Peter) Godwin as her Skipper. He was a naval officer who had been involved in the planning of this first event and had close contact with Bernard Morgan. Thanks to the auspicious enthusiasm of Earl Mountbatten, then First Sea Lord, this became possible as he guaranteed the support of the Royal Navy to organise and run the event from Torbay to Lisbon. He then appointed Captain John Illingworth, RN, to form the Race Committee, and so the races were born.

Membership of the Island Cruising Club incorporates a share in the ownership of the assets. The cost of sailing covers the upkeep of the ships, running expenses, provision of staff and administration. Formed in 1951 by Major John Baylay as a non-profit-making organisation with a special view to maintaining traditional wooden craft, it now owns a large cruising fleet including *Irina VII*, a Fife ketch, *Curlew, Casino* and *Nephalia*. It also benefits from the vessels on loan to the club—for example, *Provident* has been purchased by the Maritime Trust but will be used by the club until her sailing days are done. Accommodation is available aboard the headquarters ship *Egremont*, an ex-Liverpool ferry. On adjacent pontoons and nearby moorings, keel-boats and dinghies provide opportunities for sailing in the attractive estuary. The club provides a sound guide to seamanship, which may be harnessed to the RYA/DTI Certificate courses graduating from dinghies to yachtmasters, or simply enjoyed for the pleasure of the sport. The ICC motto is 'Don't just stand there—do something!' which means that everyone must help in running the ship, however menial the chore.

The Brixham trawler *Provident* owned by the Maritime Trust and sailed by the Island Cruising Club of Salcombe. She was built at Galmpton in 1924 *(Island Cruising Club)*

(Left to right) Gratia, Leader and *Gratitude,* owned and sailed by the Svenska Kryssarklubbens Seglarskola, the sailing school of the Swedish Cruising Association at Gothenburg *(Svenska Kryssarklubbens Seglarskola)*

Cruising, the gentle art, is a way of life—whether it is cold, wet and uncomfortable, or sunny and warm. Whether one voyages south, to Brittany and northern Spain, to the remoteness of Scottish anchorages, across the Channel—that well-oiled route—or to familiar West Country harbours, the scope is generous. Moreover, one aims to achieve each manoeuvre in a seamanlike way, and yet to give the crew a chance to learn as well. There is no age limit among the international membership of the club, which was over 3,000 in 1980.

THE RACE DIRECTOR

Later that evening I visited *Somerset*, where I found John Hamilton immersed in calculations and details for late entries. He became involved in sailing in the early sixties when, as a Royal Artillery Officer based in Germany, he answered an advertisement in the regimental magazine to sail on the gunner yacht *St Barbara* in a Tall Ships Race. This entry was organised by James Myatt at a time when John Hamilton had no knowledge of the sea, nor even how to tie a nautical hitch or a seamanlike bend.

After leaving the Army, John Hamilton spent a year as Bosun to the London Sailing Project, and then became Mate of the three-masted topsail schooner *Captain Scott*, which was built in Scotland and run by the Dulverton Trust. In 1976, while Assistant Race Director, he skippered *GBII* home from Boston for the London Sailing Project in the STA Race. He is a qualified RYA/DTI Yachtmaster examiner, and took over from Colonel Dick Scholfield as Race Director for the STA in 1976–7. He is thoroughly concerned with the race organisation and direction, and puts unstinting resourcefulness and concentration into his duties during the events. He also has to plan future races which are in the pipeline as much as ten years ahead!

I left the activity on *Somerset* to visit some other ships.

URANIA AND *EENDRACHT*

H M NL S *Urania* was built in 1928 by Haarlemsche Scheepsbouw Maatschappij as a private yacht originally called *Tromp,* with a schooner-type wishbone rig. She entered the service of the Royal Netherlands Navy in 1938, when her name was changed to *Urania* following the line of her sail-training predecessors, which had begun in 1830. She bears the motto *Caveo non timeo*—'Vigilance without fear'.

Her rig was altered in the sixties to the present-day bermudan ketch, and she carries a vast red, white and blue spinnaker in her sail wardrobe. A detailed history of *Urania* has been written by Lieutenant G. Veenman, RNLN, which will be published in Holland.

Since 1958 she has competed in almost all the STA Races, representing her country and the Royal Netherlands Navy with a crew of midshipmen cadets. She carries three officers, two petty officers and twelve cadets who usually come from the Royal Netherlands Naval College at Den Helder, where she is based for cruising from March to November each year.

That evening there was a reunion on board *Urania*, in which competitors

The Royal Netherlands naval training ketch, *Urania*, creaming along with a 'bone in her teeth'! *(Koninklijke Marine)*

reminisced about the events of past races while celebrating the Captain's birthday.

The gaff-rigged schooner *Eendracht* was built in 1974 for sail training in Holland. She was partially inspired by the Sail Training Association schooners *Sir Winston Churchill* and *Malcolm Miller* and studied their experiences. Two-week courses are run for adventure training on board. Major decisions, planning and scheduled operational costs for the ship are controlled by Het Zeilend Zeeschip, a foundation under whose authority a director is responsible for the administration. For many years this duty was performed by Hanco de Gruyter who was succeeded by Rijn Groenendijk, and later by Dan Forbes Wels.

One of the project's main inspirators was Commander H. M. Juta, who devoted much time and energy to the venture's promotion, raising funds and gaining the support necessary to run the ship. He sailed often as Captain aboard *Eendracht*, which displaces 220 tons, is 226 Thames tons, has a maximum beam of 8 metres (26 feet) and is able to carry 470 square metres of sail including the square foresail. She complies with all the regulations for Dutch safety standards and an auxiliary engine and generators have been installed under the saloon in a sound-proofed compartment. Strongly built of steel, she has weathered gales comfortably. The crew are usually volunteers, although occasionally staff have been employed. Regrettably, charges are high as costs rise with inflation. Some sponsorship of berths is available from industry, newspapers, and other organisations. The courses, which are based in Holland or northern European waters, generally last for two weeks in the summer months; in winter, courses continue in the Mediterranean where she sails with adult crews. She is fitted with heating, and the arrangement of cabin berths for twenty-six trainees enables crews to be mixed. The qualified afterguard consists of skipper, first mate, bosun, engineer, cook, instructors, watch officers, quartermasters, doctor and administrator.

A popular way of relaxing in the evening on *Eendracht* was the singing of shanties, mainly in English, to the accompaniment of the Skipper's guitar or the Mate's accordion, and the beat of the tambourine.

As the chorus lingered on the evening air I left *Urania* to explore *Carola*.

CAROLA

Carola is owned by Captain Hans-Edwin Reith who runs the family shipping company, Orion Schiffahrts-Gesellschaft Reith and Company, Johann M. K. Blumenthal Reederei, in West Germany. In 1976 a book was published to mark the seventy-fifth anniversary of the firm, which was founded in 1901 for tramptonnage work and cargoes.

Carola was built in 1900 at Nycoeping in Denmark; she was originally called *Fortuna,* then *Fauna,* later *Annemarie Grenius,* and finally *Carola*. She was originally built as a topsail schooner, but now sails as a ketch, and is modernised unobtrusively below decks.

Her hull is black, with an overall length of 25 metres (82 feet), over which she sports tan gaff sails. She is not just a bridge back to the foundation of the company when three schooners sailed under the flag of Blumenthal, but is also a complement to the beauty of sail, which the Captain and his crews perpetuate. She has participated in the Tall Ships Races since 1976 and her Captain always enters into the spirit of the occasion with zest and hospitality.

The cadets who train on board *Carola* are usually students from high schools aiming to join shipping firms when they have passed the appropriate examinations. The training is aimed at teaching them to help each other and to realise the importance of team-work. In addition, they make new connections and friendships. The courses last for four to six weeks and cadets pay only for food and linen. The ship is usually based at Travemünde and cruises throughout the summer.

MONDAY MORNING AT KIEL

At 0630 on a bright morning, with the sun catching the flags, masts and paintwork so that everything shone, all hands were ready for cleaning stations. By the time the cadets had finished polishing, the brass glowed to perfection. Sailors lined the decks ready for roll-call and inspection of uniforms. At 0800 flags were saluted while bands played, and the ensigns displaying international colours were hoisted.

The day's routine was explained by the officers, and those not on watch duties were divided into groups for tours of the city, aeroplane flights to view the scenery, visits to the HDW Shipyards, the Krupp Mak Machine Works, the Hagenuk Plant for radio communications and the television tower, or general sightseeing around the city with lunch at the Olympic Centre. These schedules were repeated the following day to include a total of 555 youngsters in the itinerary. There was also a football match against the local team. Those who went on the tours met other cadets and trainees, an important aspect of the occasion for the exchange of common experiences.

POGORIA

Early on Monday morning the Polish barquentine *Pogoria* arrived under the command of Krzysztof Baranowski, yachting author and journalist. His travels include a single-handed voyage around the world in the yacht *Polonez*, participation in *The Observer* Single-handed Transatlantic Race, and the 1976 Tall Ships Races to America when he skippered *Polonez* with a crew of young trainees. He was Master of *Zew Morza* in 1978, when he sailed from Gothenburg to Oslo via Fair Isle. In 1980 he had charge of a new ship, launched at the Gdansk Shipyard—so new, in fact, that she was still undergoing sea trials when other Polish entrants were well under way to Kiel. She was designed by Zygmunt Choreń, and it is hoped that further vessels will follow on the same lines, with possible variations of rig.

Pogoria carries fifteen permanent crew and thirty-six trainees. She is 47 metres (154 feet) overall in length and has a draught of 3.5 metres (11½ feet). Well equipped with safety gear, she is provided also for extensive cruising which could range from temperate to tropical zones. She has comprehensive radio and navigational equipment, a modern galley, refrigerators, heating and a sewage-

Pogoria, Polish barquentine launched in 1980, under sail at Bremerhaven, August 1980 *(Stadtbildstelle Seestadt Bremerhaven)*

Amphitrite, owned by Clipper Deutsches Jugendwerk zur See eV, under sail in the North Sea en route to the start of the Tall Ships Race at Gothenburg, 1978

holding tank. Safety specifications comply with the Polish Register of Shipping, Lloyd's, the Royal Ocean Racing Club and other international bodies.

This barquentine was commissioned for the Iron Shackle Fraternity, a youth opportunities scheme run through Polish television, and on her five square-sails she displays the project's emblem of four interlinked shackles. Berths on *Pogoria* are distributed as prizes for televised competitions, but she is the first vessel to be owned specifically for this purpose. Originally, prizes entailed a sailing course at Jastarnia in the Bay of Gdynia, where practical seamanship is taught in small boats for one week, followed by a cruise on larger yachts either on loan or on *Pogoria*. These courses and sailing holidays run throughout the summer for young people, but it is hoped that *Pogoria* will continue sailing in warmer climates during the winter. She has great potential and is available for charter.

On board, it was a pleasure to read the heartfelt inscriptions in her visitors' book for good luck and successful sailing. Krzysztof Baranowski wrote: 'The Iron Shackle Fraternity is following in the footsteps of the Sail Training Association and takes young people without any previous experience on offshore cruises, thus giving the chance of direct contact with the sea to those who have dreams about sailing.'

GORCH FOCK

There was great activity in the harbour as more vessels of almost every shape and size arrived. Some left to practise manoeuvres with a new crew. Everywhere people admired this gathering of eighty vessels, while the more discerning eyes appreciated every detail.

Monday was a long day for the captains who had to attend a reception given by the city president and mayor in the Town Hall. Later, a second reception took place aboard the West German naval barque *Gorch Fock II* which the Press attended. *Gorch Fock II* was built in 1958 by the famous Blohm and Voss Shipyard of Hamburg which had launched her predecessor and other training barques to similar design in the 1930s. *Gorch Fock I* was, in fact, built in 1933 to replace the jackass barque *Niobe* which had foundered with much loss of life in a sudden lightning squall in the Baltic Sea in 1932. After World War II she was taken over by the USSR and now sails as *Tovarisch*, which since 1977 has been confined to the Black and Mediterranean Seas. She is a sister ship to two barques which were built for the German Navy by Blohm and Voss, the *Horst Wessel*, now called *Eagle* and owned by the United States Coast Guard, and *Sagres II*, originally *Albert Leo Schlageter*, now of the Portuguese Navy. The Rumanian barque *Mircea II* was also built to the same plans.

Gorch Fock II complies with the highest standards of safety regulations especially instrumented after the tragic loss in 1957 of the four-masted barque *Pamir* with nearly all hands while en route to Europe from Australia with a cargo of grain.

The barque is named after the naval poet Johann Kinau who wrote under the pseudonym Gorch Fock. The objective on board is to train young officer and petty officer candidates while introducing them to different countries.

Her captains, who are much respected in the world of sail training, have maintained a handsome reputation for the barque. In 1980 in command was Captain Horst Wind, whose predecessors have included Captain Hans Engel, the representative of the STA in West Germany, Captain H. von Stackelberg and Captain Ernst von Witzendorff. She has participated in the Tall Ships Races on many occasions, winning the races in 1962 from Torbay to Rotterdam, in 1968 from Gothenburg to Kristiansand via an oil-rig in the North Sea, and, on a similar course in 1978, from Gothenburg around Fair Isle, when she led by a large margin on the return to Oslo. On one memorable occasion during the London Festival of Sail in 1975 she sailed out from her berth under Tower Bridge.

DANMARK

I joined *Danmark* in Kiel and, having been shown a berth, unpacked my gear and been guided around the decks, began to make my way ashore. Before I had crossed the gangway, however, whistles announced the arrival of Captain Arntsen, Master of *Sørlandet*, Captain Bentsen, Master of *Danmark*, and others. They all came on board and I was invited to join them in the saloon aft. Gleaming french-polished mahogany greeted us, classic in its simplicity; only two portraits, that of Queen Margrethe of Denmark and her husband, Prince Henrik, cover any portion of the wood panelling. Delicate curtains interwoven with the name of the ship subdue the source of natural light. In such a place where many seamen have talked and conversation naturally flowed, I learnt of the value placed by the Danish Government in *Danmark*:

'On a yard-arm a hundred feet above the deck a boy learns self-reliance and develops a sense of responsibility, knowing that his shipmates beside him and on deck below expect of him the care and precision that will ensure their safety. For developing these qualities a period on a training ship is worth any amount of money—which is no doubt the chief reason why sailing ships are still used for training today.'

The conversation developed into an account by Bentsen and Arntsen of the 1960 Tall Ships Race from Oslo to Ostend when their ships were engaged in a close tacking competition after they had met up during the first few days of the race. From then on, it was tack for tack, following close on each other's heels for every manoeuvre until the last moments of the finish when *Sørlandet* crossed the line ahead, weathering the mark. In fact, *Statsraad Lehmkuhl* from Norway had actually won that race.

Captain B. Barner Jespersen, Master of *Georg Stage*, a cheerful character with a slight gingery beard, talked of his fine ship, a miniature, well-proportioned full-

Tovarisch (ex-*Gorch Fock I*) preparing to set sail at the start of the 1976 Tall Ships Race, from Tenerife to Bermuda. She is now owned by the Kherson Marine School, in the USSR, based on the Black Sea

Gorch Fock II owned by the West German Navy, under way at Bremerhaven, August 1980, when she was celebrating the anniversary of her namesake (*Stadtbildstelle Seestadt Bremerhaven*)

rigger, and the training aboard her. She is thoroughly sailed throughout the Baltic and North Seas, and through the years she and her predecessor, later to become *Joseph Conrad*, have sailed and trained thousands of boys in preparation for the Danish Merchant Navy.

I asked him what his views were on using sailing ships to educate sailors today. He replied as follows:

'Nowadays, the aim is not to teach the cadets to sail a sailing vessel. The ship is not the goal, but the means of reaching the goal of educating and teaching proper behaviour at sea. A sailing ship has many advantages which do not exist on a motor vessel or at a land-based school. These advantages are:

'1   The ship is a good educational tool. Young people are put into a new situation where they must co-operate with the crew and follow their instructions. This rapidly influences the theoretical guidance, where the teachers (the officers) have the advantage that the students must listen to and obey them, learning the hard way. It quickly teaches co-operation. Group dynamics and other psychological tricks are not necessary on a sailing ship.

'Practically, there is always essential work to do and no need to invent tasks which will be scrapped afterwards. This gives students a different type of interest which other educational institutions cannot provide.

'The aspect of physical exercise is automatically catered for on board a full-rigged ship. There is no need for a football pitch or a gymnasium, and there is always lots of fresh air.

'2   Socially, one always finds something extra from the ship. Many young people today are frustrated because they cannot overlook the society in which they are living. They cannot see where they fit into the large complicated social structure. A ship is a minor society where young people can learn how their own behaviour and that of others may influence everyone. They can see their own position and its meaning to the rest of the crew and the running of the ship. This gives them peace and self-confidence, so that at the end of the voyage they have the ship's organisation as a model and are able to examine the rest of society.

'When many people are assembled in a small area like a sailing ship, they must be even more aware and considerate of others than when on shore. A full-rigged ship has a large crew and therefore demands the highest level of consideration . It is not long before they learn that if they treat their companions with respect, they will be treated respectfully in return. The situation is such that they must act socially in order to survive. The phrase "To lend the man next to you a hand when uninvited, and without asking anything in return", is not meaningless but evident in everyday behaviour. This attitude remains with young sailors for life, and they will become good shipmates.

'3   The experience of life under sail in varying weather conditions gives the students an insight into many of nature's peculiar ways. The fact that the ship is moving from place to place gives a break in daily routine which makes school-time more interesting. In other words, picnics and excursions are unnecessary to break the grey days.

'Besides these obvious advantages concerning the sailing vessel, the ship is such

Twin French naval topsail schooners, *Belle Poule* and *Etoile*

a vital part of our culture that we have to preserve it for the coming generations, and the best way to do so is to continue sailing. If all the square-riggers were laid up as museum pieces, and if sailing knowledge was only to be read about in books, our thousand-year-old maritime traditions and experience would be lost forever—and the world would be a much poorer place.'

Of course, not all sail-training ships are run for the merchant navies—for instance, alongside *Danmark* lay HMS *Falken* of the Royal Swedish Navy. I was introduced to her Captain, Lieutenant Ragnar Westblad, who was among the company and who told me something about the history of sail training in the Swedish Navy.

HMS *FALKEN* AND HMS *GLADAN*

The Royal Swedish Navy was founded in 1556 by King Gustaf Wasa. Regular

57

sail training was first established in 1776 with the navy brig *Diana*. Since then, thirty vessels have succeeded her in this duty, maintaining an unbroken line of tradition.

In 1877 the brig *Falken*, 115 tons, was commissioned for training duty. She made cruises throughout the summer in the Baltic Sea. Later, she was joined in this work by the full-rigged ships *Najaden* and *Jarramas*. They were designed for the Swedish Navy on similar lines with the characteristics of small sailing frigates: both had a displacement of 350 tons, and were 33 metres (108 feet) length overall. *Najaden* was built of wood in 1897, and *Jarramas* of iron in 1900. They sailed together throughout the Baltic on short training cruises, and across the North Sea, often in company with *Falken*, until she was sold in 1944. Shortly afterwards, *Najaden* was bought on her retirement by the town of Halmstad and she still lies smartly maintained there, alongside the quay. *Jarramas* retired from the Royal Swedish Navy in 1948 and was purchased by the town of Karlskrona, where she still lies in 1980. As a replacement for these vessels, the twin gaff schooners *Gladan* and *Falken* were commissioned in 1947, since when they have sailed in the Baltic and North Seas and across the Atlantic. Each of these attractive schooners carries 28 cadets, aged from 17 to 22 years, for courses of usually 3–5 weeks. There are also 6–8 crew and 8 officers on board.

Since the first Tall Ships Race in 1956, both *Falken* and *Gladan* have gained a reputation for good sailing qualities and their officers and boys are noted for their competitive spirit. In 1956 *Falken* was fourth and *Gladan* sixth in class. For the Gothenburg to Kristiansand race in 1968 *Gladan* gained first prize in class and overall, while *Falken* was second, placings which were repeated in the 1972 Helsingfors to Malmö race. In 1975, in the race from IJmuiden to Den Helder, it was *Falken* which gained the honours, while *Gladan* was second. During the 1976 series across the Atlantic *Gladan* came second in class and sixth overall on three out of the four races organised by the STA. Her Captain on that occasion was Commander Sten Gattberg, one of the Chief Liaison Officers in Karlskrona in 1980. The Silver Jubilee Race to Le Havre after the Fleet Review at Spithead in 1977 was won by *Gladan*, with *Falken*, close astern, second in class. In 1978 *Gladan*, sailed by Lt-Commander Claes Öquist, was awarded the Cutty Sark Trophy for International Understanding, a recognition which complemented the consistent friendship shown by these two vessels throughout the years.

Naturally, when the two schooners race together not only do they present a fine appearance in duplicate, but they generate an intership rivalry. Sadly, in 1980 *Gladan* was unable to grace the starting lines as she was laid up mastless in Karlskrona. HMS *Falken*, however, represented the Royal Swedish Navy in admirable style.

THE SWEDISH CRUISING ASSOCIATION
Alongside the quay lay two ships owned by the Swedish Cruising Association: *Gratia of Gothenburg*, skippered by a young naval officer, Gösta af Klint, and the West Country trawler ketch *Gratitude of Gothenburg*, skippered by Kjell Wollter, a great sailing character whose smile radiates from a sun-tanned face which

HMS *Gladan*, sister ship to HMS *Falken*, gaff schooners launched in 1947 for the Royal Swedish Navy *(Commander Sten Gattberg, RSN)*

'I spy a tall ship!' Captain Ragnar Westblad aboard HMS *Falken*. *Sørlandet* in the background

contrasts with his silvered hair. His career began in 1934–5 when he sailed on board the Swedish four-masted barque *Abraham Rydberg*, on which he was later an AB. He also sailed as Chief Officer on Lord Runciman's *Sunbeam II* which was later bought by the Rydberg Foundation for training boys at sea. Her name was then changed to *Flying Clipper* and she competed in the first Tall Ships Race. Although Kjell Wollter served as a regular officer in the Merchant Marine he sailed whenever possible. In 1968–9 he was Master of the privately owned *Antarna* (now called *Sea Cloud*) and sailed her from Naples to the Virgin Isles, Miami, the Bahamas, Mexico, and elsewhere.

The Sailing School for the Swedish Cruising Association was founded in 1957 by a few enthusiastic people in Gothenburg under the initiation of Kjell Wollter, Master Pilot Harald Palmquist, and Sven Lignell who discovered *Gratitude* as almost a wreck lying at Hönö, Sweden. She was built as a trawler at Porthleven, Cornwall, in 1907, but had been based in Sweden since 1932. Having bought her, they restored her and she began sailing again in 1959, this time as a training ship.

Leader of Gothenburg was not present at Kiel. She had come second in 1978 in the Tall Ships Race from Gothenburg around Fair Isle to Oslo, which *Gratitude* actually won with an all-female crew of trainees. *Leader*, another sailing trawler, was launched in Galmpton on the River Dart in Devon in 1892, as was *Provident* of the Island Cruising Club in 1924. She worked in Sweden from 1907, and was found lying at Sannäs in 1969. The Swedish Cruising Association then renovated her and have used her as a training ship since 1973.

Gratia, originally *Blue Shadow*, was built in Britain in 1900 for a lord whose son sailed her to Denmark, where he sold her. In 1936 the Swedish ship-owner Einar Hansen bought her and changed her name to *Cinderella*. He sailed her as his private yacht until 1964, when he donated her to the Swedish Cruising Association, which painted her hull blue, in line with their club colours.

The trainees are either all-male or all-female groups, and the cruises run through the summer, usually based from Gothenburg and sailing in Scandinavian waters. All the qualified staff on board are volunteers, 90 per cent having started as cadets with the club.

The ships are sailed and maintained in a seamanlike way, although the sheer pleasure of cruising, especially in the island-studded Scandinavian waters, is never forgotten. Life on board is experienced each season by about 1,000 youngsters and 200 senior cadets (adult courses are run in spring and autumn). The three ships accumulate 10,000 nautical miles each year, but there are no written manuals or histories of the club for, as they say: 'We sail more than we write.' The administration is run by two part-time secretaries in Gothenburg, while all maintenance and winter-work is completed as much as possible by volunteers who have sailed on the ships.

Not only has Captain Kjell Wollter generated the enthusiasm which inspires the Swedish Cruising Association and skippered its ships each summer for the past twenty-two years, but he has recently instigated a project to build a new vessel which, in his own words, will be 'My testimony to the young people of Sweden.' She is being built during 1980–1 on the lines of a traditional Brixham trawler, but will be fitted with a layout similar to that of the present-day *Gratitude*. Her length overall will be 25 metres (83 feet) and she will be built of wood at the Karstensens Skibvaerft at Skagen in northern Denmark, a yard which specialises in wooden ship-building and repairs, as well as working on steel ships. It was the success of *Gratitude* under Wollter's command, when he sailed with female trainees in 1978 on the Gothenburg to Oslo STA Tall Ships Race, that helped to raise the support for building this new wooden gaff ketch.

Could another group of girls help to repeat that success on the race to Karlskrona in 1980?

Meanwhile, *Gratia* had boys on board, except for some of the crew. The First Mate was Maria Björnstam, the first woman to qualify as a Master Mariner in the Swedish Merchant Navy, and a keen supporter of the SCA yachts and the value of sail training. The Second Mate's sister was sailing aboard as cook.

THE CAPTAIN'S DINNER

On the last night in harbour at Kiel a captain's dinner was provided, with entertainment by the Kiel Pilots Choir, whose admirable rendering of shanties was aided in the choruses by the company. This traditional occasion provides the opportunity for discussions before the race on the art of sailing—the techniques, innovations and related skills. Canvas versus dacron, hemp and manilla versus terylene and other artificial fibres, bunks versus hammocks, and many more intricate and important details are discussed in the conversations, which also provide the opportunity for reminiscences, introductions and meetings, leading to the camaraderie and friendships of the events. So, as the crews united, they were bound into a family, 'the family of man, an harmonious group linked together by common interest', proving, as a Polish journalist said in 1974, that 'the sea can be our bridge'.

This extensive family has a respected father in Lieutenant-Commander The Honourable Greville Howard, VRD, RNR, who, since the races began, has devoted time, energy and resources to the events. He appreciates the international value of the occasions and makes every effort to contribute to its success, personally greeting every ship which competes.

During World War II he served in the Royal Naval Reserve aboard an MTB, destroyers, 'Q' ships, and later on frigates, spending most of the time at sea. He became Mayor of Westminster in 1946–7, when he was also Assistant County Commissioner for the Sea Scouts in London. He stood as the Member of Parliament for the St Ives District of Cornwall 1950–66, when he retired. Since then, he has been an Honorary Overseas Director and European consultant of a colour processing laboratory, and is an excellent photographer himself. As well as being Chairman of the Sail Training Association, Sailing Overseas, he is an Honorary Vice-President of the Royal National Lifeboat Institution, and the Honorary Joint President of the National Association of Inshore Fishermen. He believes in giving young people of many nationalities the chance to meet through sail-training competitions, organised in the spirit of the camaraderie of the sea which he exemplifies during the races.

Captain Hans Engel, enthusiastic promoter of sail training in West Germany, stands by The Hon Greville Howard (affectionately known as 'Father' to the fleet of tall ships) while he talks to a ship during the Windjammer Parade at Kiel, 1972 *(Henryk Kabat, Gdynia)*

Prize-giving at the Ostseehalle, Kiel; *(left to right)* Miguel, a cadet from *Guayas*, holding Cutty Sark Friendship Trophy, Captain Nelson Armas, the Skipper of *Lindø*, and Captain John Martin with two cadets from *Blanca Estela (D. J. Benstead)*

Known and addressed by many of the fleet captains simply as 'Father', there can be few who have ever had so many close relations, whether at ports visited throughout the races or among the thousands of people worldwide who have sailed with the tall ships during past STA events. By 1980 the races will have taken place for nearly 25 years, visited many different ports and harbours, while having covered over 25,000 nautical miles under sail and enabled more than 60,000 sailors to participate aboard a diversity of ships representing at least 25 different countries with crews from twice that number of nationalities.

Each competitor will have his or her own memories over the years, but at Kiel there was one outstanding event. One evening, many of the 3,000 cadets and trainees from all the ships, along with the captains, officers, cooks, bosuns and officials, were invited to the Ostseehalle.

THE OSTSEEHALLE
The evening began with the prize-giving for the race from Boston, USA, to Kristiansand, Norway. Cadets, trainees and officers from all the ships were there to see Vice-Admiral Weschler, USN (Retd), present the prizes. First prize in Class A was received by Commander Jan Fjeld Hansen, Master of the *Christian Radich*, who had travelled from Oslo on behalf of the ship. Captain Horst Wind received

second prize for *Gorch Fock II*. Third prize went to Captain Nelson Armas for *Guayas*, which was awarded also the Cutty Sark Friendship Trophy, the ASTA Race equivalent to the Cutty Sark Trophy, both regarded as the epitome of these events. The award is voted for by all the competing captains for the ship which they feel has shown the greatest goodwill towards international friendship and understanding. The openness and hospitality of *Guayas'* crew was illustrated by the following words by one of the officers on board: 'Our ship is tied to your quay, and our hearts are tied to your people.' In Class B first prize went to *Christian Venturer* of Bermuda, second to *Lindφ* and third to *Blanca Estela* from Chile.

The 3,000 cadets, trainees, officers and officials were packed into the massive hall. Among the guests were representatives from the welcoming party from Karlskrona, including Sonnie Nilsson and Torsten Wikström, and the crews, captains and cadets from *Gratia, Gratitude, Kranich, Somerset, Chwan,* whose home port is Karlskrona, *Elinor* from Denmark, and *Zebu*, with girl trainees from the Avon area Sea Rangers in Britain, skippered by Peter Hambly who has described the 1976 series of STA Races in *Race Under Sail*. There was *Walross III* from West Germany, whose crew had received a showering of flour-bombs from the enthusiastic LSP trainees of *GBII* in the Parade of Sail at Boston Harbour in 1976. On that occasion *Walross III* had been sailing beautifully under spinnaker when she was surprised by *GBII* but she retaliated later, when she beat up close behind the large red ketch to hand over a liquid present concealed in a bottle. *GBII* was at that time captained by 'Rule Britannia' Myatt.

There was an exciting atmosphere as the music, dancing and conversation began. The band from *Guayas* played Latin American rhythms by request, interspersed between pop music and jazz, all of which proved popular, judging by the activity on the dance floor. The dancing continued into the night, as did the conversations. The friendships had begun.

4

THE PARADE OF SAIL

Do you know the shallow Baltic where the seas
are steep and short,
Where the bluff, lee-boarded fishing luggers ride?

RUDYARD KIPLING, 'Feet of the Young Men'

The day of the Parade of Sail out of Kiel was overcast, with rain clouds blown by a southerly wind. Umbrellas crowded the pavements, masking the onlookers who were not deterred by the persistent rain. People sheltered under trees and gazed up at the tall masts waiting to depart. Everything—flags, sails and booms—was drenched by the inhospitable downpour.

POLISH ENTRIES IN CLASS B

As I made my way along the quay, I passed some of the Class B III vessels. Some were competitors from Poland, keen supporters of the races, entered through the Polish Yachting Association. *Hajduk*, a 25-ton TM bermudan sloop, is owned by M. K. S. Pogon, while her sister ship *Trygław* (named after a pre-Christian Polish god with three faces), had sailed from the Merchant Navy Academy at Szczecin which owns her for training. *Roztocze*, under the command of Ziemowit Baranski, was built in 1969 at Szczecin for the Lublin District Yachting Association. Since she was launched, she has averaged about five months' sailing each year, mainly in the Baltic and North Sea, but has also ventured as far south as the Mediterranean and the Black Sea, and as far north as a circumnavigation of Iceland. She has visited nineteen countries, sailed 73,931 nautical miles, and trained 1,075 young people. Since Lublin lies about 420 kilometres (260 miles) from the sea it is particularly important for the association to have its own vessel for its members.

Wodnik II (named after the pre-Christian Polish god of water), a 19-ton TM bermudan ketch owned by Zwiazek Harcerstwa Polskiego, was another entrant. Near her lay *Wojewoda Pomorski*, entered by the Students Yacht Club. She is a large bermudan sloop, 45 tons TM, which had entered the races previously in 1978.

And there was *Hetman* under the command of Jan Pinkiewicz, who had sailed her in the STA Races of 1974, when she was fifth in her class, the Atlantic series from Bermuda to Newport when she came second in her class, and in 1978. Built in Bremen in 1936 for a club in Gdynia and rebuilt in 1966, this yacht annually makes two or three long cruises and a few short trips along the Polish coast. She is

The German gaff cutter *Gronland*, built in 1867, and restored by volunteers for her owners, the Deutsches Schiffahrtsmuseum (*Wolfhard Scheer, Nordsee-Zeitung*)

owned by the Kotwica Yacht Club at Gdynia, and carries four cadets aged from 19 to 24 years and three officers on behalf of the Polish Yachting Association and the Yacht Club. These young people come from the Naval Academy, and other high schools, but not necessarily to train for a career at sea.

DEPARTURE

Gradually the ships left Kiel and disappeared into the misty rain in the fiord. First the smaller vessels, gaffers, schooners and ketches, which did not require the assistance of tugs, set off to find their designated places. In this parade the Class B vessels were interspersed between the Class A square-riggers.

Later in the morning, we stood by on board *Danmark* to leave our berth. We were last in the line of square-riggers as the others had undocked from a nearby quay before us. We viewed *Sørlandet, Dar Pomorza* and the newly launched *Pogoria* through the mist as they passed us under the pilot's eyes. As *Pogoria* passed by, her crew lined up on deck and the cadets waved at us.

Outside us HMS *Falken* moved away with the assistance of tugs; we waved farewell to her crew who were clad in red oilskins.

As our turn to join the parade approached, we waved goodbye to Finn Bergmann, Director of *Danmark* and the STA's Danish representative who had been visiting the ship in Kiel, and watched the lines of spectators diminish as we drew away. We waited our turn as the Class B vessels in our group assembled beside us; there was the *Eendracht* from the Netherlands, *Gratia* and *Gratitude* from Sweden, and many more, some with sails raised in preparation for the parade. Astern of us *Sea Cloud*, setting topsails, stood by to bring up the rear.

GRØNLAND AND *ASTARTE*

We passed close by the *Gronland*, grandfather of the fleet, now owned by the Deutsches Schiffahrtsmuseum. Built in 1867 for polar exploration, she has been beautifully restored by a group of volunteers from the city of Bremerhaven to maintain her in sailing trim. She is rigged as a gaff cutter with the addition of two yards with square-sails. Her Master was Captain Manfred Hövener, who was involved in her restoration, and her trainees were students from Bremerhaven Polytechnic who sail with her during the summer. Her motto is: 'We are all sitting in one boat and must stick together!' The trainees are known for their singing of shanties when, clothed in matching striped smocks, they are accompanied by the Mate, Gunther Bockelmann, on his accordion.

Another vessel in our group was the Finkenwerder cutter *Astarte*, owned by the Schiffergilde of Bremerhaven eV, a public charity founded in 1978 to preserve and rescue the last sailing commercial ships of the north German coastal region and to teach maritime traditions and customs to the younger generation through sail training. In the year it was founded the gilde purchased *Astarte* and then spent two years rebuilding her so that she was the same fishing vessel that had been built in 1903 in a small village near Hamburg, but fitted out with cabins instead of a hold. Having been accurately restored, she participated in the race to Karlskrona in 1980, skippered by Klaus Walter Rode, with Harald von Forstner as Mate, known to many through his own vessel *Winny* and through sailing *Tina IV* in 1976.

TS *ROYALIST*

Royalist then sailed close by us—*Mini-Kruzenshtern*, as she was called by the Russians, owing to her black hull and painted gun-ports. As she bowled along in the grey-green seas it was possible to recognise the Sailing Master, Geoff Ullrich, Bosun Trevor, and the engineer, coxswain and cook who comprise the permanent crew of this brig which is owned by the Sea Cadet Corps in Britain. The inspiration for building her in 1971 came from the success of the brigantine *Centurion* in the Tall Ships Race of 1966 from Falmouth to Copenhagen. On loan from her owner, *Centurion* had sailed with a crew of sea cadets under the command of Lieutenant-Commander Morin Scott, RNR, and won her class. This prompted the Sea Cadet Corps to consider owning a vessel for sail training, and plans were drawn up by the yacht designer Colin Mudie, in liaison with Lieutenant-Commander Scott. She is 24 metres (78 feet) length overall, is 110 tons TM (48 tons displacement), is built of steel, and sails from March to November on weekly cruises, usually based from Gosport. She takes sea cadets and members of the Girls Nautical Training Corps to sea for a tough, rigorous

The gaff ketch *Astarte*, owned by the Schiffergilde Bremerhaven eV *(left)*, and the three-masted gaff schooner *Elinor*, owned by Palle Blinkenberg of Denmark *(right)* *(Stadtbildstelle Seestadt Bremerhaven)*

Royalist creaming along under full sail *(print courtesy of Sea Cadet Corps, copyright the Daily Telegraph)*

training, and her design has proved thoroughly successful for this purpose. Each summer she takes over 800 youngsters to sea. She carries 22 cadets, 6 officers and 4 additional volunteer crew. Although not all cadets will join the Royal Navy, it is hoped that all receive a good grounding in seamanship. This active brig has the support of the Square Rigger Club which helps to provide funds and gifts, as well as sponsoring berths. Her motto, emblazoned on her bow, is: 'Ready, Aye, Ready.'

Royalist is fully equipped with safety gear and when she was launched in 1971 she was awarded the Lloyd's Register Yacht Award. For Race One in 1980, her Master was Morin Scott, from behind whose skilfully trimmed silver beard emanates a warm smile. He is a character seldom without a yarn, and is thoroughly immersed in sail training and seafaring schemes, is Commodore of the Square-Rigger Club, a long-standing member of the Royal Cruising Club, and is greatly involved in the Jubilee Trust Project to build a barque for the handicapped.

THE PARADE

Every variety of craft came to see the ships, from dinghies, wind-surfers and yachts to motor-vessels and cruisers. The crowds on shore occupied every inch of space with a view—some spectators were even knee-deep in water.

We passed the official spectator boat *Funny Girl*, where we saluted the officials of Kiel and the STA. The vessels began to spread out with *Gorch Fock* sailing at 11 knots, leading the parade. We slowed down for the pilot to disembark before continuing towards the anchorage. The wind increased and some of the smaller vessels had a rough passage to Falster, many taking shelter in Gedser, where a number had to make repairs. Other vessels also had problems, some of which were solved before the start, others which were not.

Captain Bentsen peered from beneath his deep sou'wester. The Chief Mate, Knud Vang Nielsen, stood alongside him. We were on our way. Near the galley, Daniel the Bosun, 'Bose' as the boys called him, was serving a splice with the help of some of the cadets, while other oilskin-clad sailors walked cautiously about the wet, dark teak decks.

DANMARK

The full-rigged ship *Danmark* was launched in 1933 for the Danish Government at the Nakskov Shipyard in Lolland. She was designed by Aage Larsen, constructed of steel and is 845 Thames tons, 790 gross registered tons, and 65 metres (213 feet) length overall. The Danes have a tradition of training good seamen and the aim on board *Danmark* is to provide courses for future merchant sailors.

In 1939 she sailed to New York for the World's Trade Fair and was there when war broke out. Many of her cadets joined the Allied Forces, while the ship was loaned to the United States Coast Guard until 1945. During these years 5,000 cadets benefited from life aboard *Danmark* and the US Coast Guard Service was reluctant to part with her. Naturally, the Danes wanted her back, so another ship, the Blohm and Voss barque *Horst Wessel*, was taken from the German

Navy as reparations and replaced *Danmark* in the USA. *Horst Wessel* was renamed *Eagle* and still sails today.

Danmark, having returned to her home base, continued to take boys on five-month courses across the seas of northern Europe, to the Mediterranean, the Caribbean and North America, where she is always received warmly and with great interest. She sailed with 120 cadets until 1959 when, after an extensive refit, her capacity was reduced to 80 in order to provide better accommodation. The ship has a remarkable line of captains who have always been concerned for their cadets. From 1937 Captain Knud L. Hansen sailed her, remaining as a senior officer with a US Coast Guard captain while she was in the United States. He resumed his position from 1945 to 1964 when he was taken ill in New York after the Tall Ships Race across the Atlantic. This race, from Lisbon to Bermuda, was organised by the STA and finished with a Parade of Sail in New York Harbour. Under his command, the ship gained a reputation for skilful manoeuvring under sail, which she has never lost and many harbours have been enhanced by her graceful handling. Since 1964 Captain Wilhelm Hansen has been one of her masters. In 1976 she sailed into St George's Harbour, Bermuda, through the extremely narrow entrance, to the admiration of bystanders— a superb feat of seamanship executed without fuss.

Each year Captain Wilhelm Hansen takes one of the five-month courses. In 1980 he sailed with *Danmark* from January until early July, when Captain Otto L. Bentsen took over for the second half of the year at Aalborg, and entered the Cutty Sark Tall Ships Race to Karlskrona.

FALSTER

We sailed on to the starting area, passing *Le Papillon*, a green American schooner of 34 Thames tons sailed over from the United States by Tom Lemm, who built her, and D. L. with a young crew. Although it appeared from our steady decks that she was rolling considerably on the increasing seas, she was in fact in no difficulty.

By 1600 we had travelled about 21 miles and were out of Kiel Bay. We arrived at the Fehmarn Belt Lightship at 1830, after another 20 miles, steering almost due east. The Fehmarn Belt prevented the race from starting offshore from Kiel, as this narrow strip of water between the island of Lolland to the north and Fehmarn to the south contains the invisible Danish–German borders and is strictly buoyed for navigation.

Having passed the Gedser Reef, south of Falster, we sailed approximately 63 miles before we neared the anchorage at 0300 on 17 July, which was the proposed day of the start. Those who were off duty now climbed into their hammocks and slept until the day watches were called again. The wind stirred in the rigging, catching the shrouds and playing a tune. It blew from the west across the low-lying sandy beaches and land composed of grass and dunes. In that direction, on the far side of Lolland beyond Falster, lay the Nakskov Shipyard, where *Danmark* had been built in 1932–3, and where, in 1930, *Dar Pomorza* was recommissioned for training in Poland. Since it was founded in 1916, over 200 vessels have been

The full-rigged ship *Danmark* alongside at Oslo after the Tall Ships Race in 1978

built at the yard which is still busy constructing advanced cargo liners, container carriers, ferries, super-ferries and tankers. *Dar Pomorza* revisited Nakskov in 1980 to mark the fiftieth anniversary of her Polish career. During her stay, one of the former directors of the yard, Otto Petersen, wrote in the red leather-bound visitors' book which is always on board the ship: 'I always remember *Dar Pomorza* as our ideal ship, when we, at Nakskov, later built the training ship *Danmark*.'

AT ANCHOR

Other lights showed vessels at anchor around us. *Somerset*, to the north of us, kept guard to prevent anyone from wandering into the zone near to shore where fishing nets lay unmarked, and she warned approaching ships of this recent navigational hazard by radio or flashing lights. During the night, ships continued arriving after the passage from Kiel, while others took shelter en route at Gedser. Some, like *Blue Sirius*, encountered serious problems and had to return to harbour. A crew member of *Zebu* was injured. *British Soldier* and *Dasher* had damaged sails and a mast track, and returned to Kiel for repairs; not realising the situation of the race, both missed the start and sailed direct to Karlskrona.

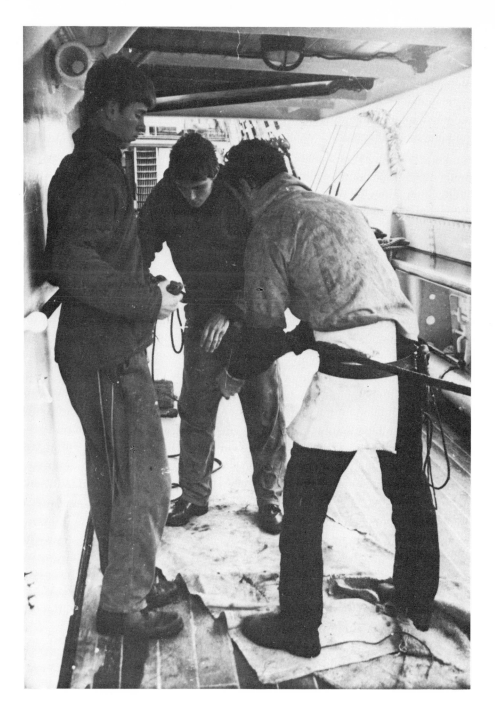

Danmark's Bosun wearing a protective apron of sailcloth, serves a splice with the help of two cadets

At dawn there was a strong squally wind and the forecast predicted worsening conditions. The meteorologists indicated that most likely there would be gale-force winds from south-west to west, occasionally gusting Force 9. The start was delayed for six hours.

For the square-riggers, eager to start, this postponement was unfavourable. The wind was to their advantage, presenting no danger of gybing as it would to fore-and-aft vessels. However, the smaller ships and the young untrained crews had to be considered and now, as the fleet waited, everyone was informed of the situation over the VHF radio.

In sight, other vessels lay at anchor—*Sørlandet*, *Royalist*, *Gorch Fock* and others—while throughout the morning *Kruzenshtern* steamed up and down offshore. The Royal Danish Navy vessels which were to start the race were anchored to the north, and the Danish officers could be heard on the air during the day. At times the sun shone, highlighting the breaking white crests of the waves over the shallow green water.

The wind whipped around the ship unpleasantly for the boys busy changing a sail out on the bowsprit. It was a cold exhilarating day but on deck the boys worked at sail repairs, splicing and serving.

The Bosun is always busy with shipboard maintenance, the repair and care of ropes, running rigging and paintwork and, under his watchful eye, the boys scraped, prepared and primed any apparent rust on deck and stripped and painted their wash-room. Maintenance duties were performed all round, while the Bosun himself, apart from supervising, prepared a serving, tar dripping on to his protective apron, while two cadets observed and assisted him. On *Danmark* many traditional seafaring skills are still used for practical purposes, and the standard of seamanship is very high. Ropes are constantly checked, and replaced when necessary, gear and rigging watched for chafe and overhauled, sails are repaired, or a flying jib removed from the bowsprit for a stitch or two. The Bosun must be exemplary in his skills.

Later, he sat on a bench on deck to sew strips of canvas into riggers' bags which would be presented at the end of the course to the most outstanding cadets. He instructed me in the art, so I made a similar bag from canvas with a wooden bottom provided by the carpenter. At the end of the race I was formally presented with suitable contents for this important item of traditional seaman's gear.

The present cadets, having successfully completed a course ashore, had all been sent from Danish shipping companies as part of their training, with all costs paid for them. In January, in Majorca, the boys had spent the first weeks of the cruise rigging the ship, sending up the upper yards, bending on sails, while learning about the gear and its uses. This familiarisation is an all-important part of the training. Then it was time to set sail across the Atlantic to the United States via the Caribbean, where at anchor they caught a large shark, and, later in the Bahamas, took a smaller one. The first was 3.5 metres ($11\frac{1}{2}$ feet) long and took some hoisting on board. Its mouthful of teeth provided almost everyone on board with a memento! The Captain had a stick made out of the backbone, and, as a good-luck charm, the tail adorned the bowsprit and the fins the foremast.

The normal study programme continued all the way, and the cadets had to learn navigation, English, Rules of the Road, seamanship and other subjects organised by Knud Vang Nielsen, the Chief Instructor (who became Chief Mate during the race in the Baltic), a young seaman with an accurate eye for the set of the sails. Lectures on subjects ranging from lifeboat drill and safety to engines and generators were given by the officers, and studies were supplemented by correspondence courses. Ship, sails and deck had to be cared for during watches and sail exercises, and, having sailed over 14,000 nautical miles on a square-rigger, the cadets gained a thorough knowledge of their ship. After their voyage on *Danmark* they would complete further studies and examinations towards careers in the Danish Merchant Navy.

After the long six-month voyage, the thought of nearing home gave rise to excitement, although it was tinged with tiredness. The ship had, in fact, stopped in Denmark, but only for a couple of days at Aalborg—just long enough to tantalise the desire to see families and friends.

Weather conditions were still being discussed when a message was received over the radio: the start of the race was to be delayed further—Class A was to commence at 0700 on the following morning, 18 July.

5

DANMARK IN THE BALTIC

On a rather hurried trip round the Baltic during the late summer of 1937, I was surprised to see six full-rigged ships in one week. They were all schoolships—the small Swedish naval schoolships Najaden *and* Jarramas, *which were lying at anchor off Harwich as the Esbjerg motor-ship took me to sea; the Danish schoolship* Georg Stage, *at anchor for the night off Korsør in Denmark; the Danish Government's full-rigger* Danmark, *under sail near the same place; the Norwegian* Sørlandet, *off Kristiansand, and the Polish* Dar Pomorza, *off Gdynia. Later, on the same trip I saw the Oslo full-rigger* Christian Radich, *launched in May of this year, and the German* Gorch Fock *in the distance.*

As for other square-riggers there were scarcely any . . .

ALAN VILLIERS, The Making of a Sailor (1937)

From 0500 on the day of the start coffee was served in the galley. Then, with the call to up-anchor, the engine throbbed into life. An hour later we were preparing to set sail. The cadets were aloft releasing gaskets, bunt-lines and clew-lines; on deck, coils of rope were ready to run. Yards were braced, halliards ready and sheets led correctly as all the ships neared the starting line—closer than they would be again before reaching Karlskrona—and soon all began to set sail. On a square-rigger like *Danmark* setting sail is a gradual process—as each sail is hoisted and the wind force harnessed, so the ship's speed increases.

At 0625 we set our lower and upper topsails on all masts. Ten minutes later the topgallants were set and only two minutes after that, high aloft, the royals. Cadets worked the sails in unison on deck amid a sea of hemp and manilla.

As we gained speed we neared the Russian four-masted barque *Kruzenshtern*. She lay on our port side, beyond *Dar Pomorza* and *Gorch Fock*. Dipping ensigns, we lined the decks to admire this huge well-proportioned vessel as she continued to set her sails, seams straining under the pressure of the wind. Her size, 3,064 gross registered tons, 3,185 Thames tons, contrasted with the Danish full-rigger *Georg Stage* of only 298 gross registered tons and 396 Thames tons.

Although helicopters roared above the scene, few spectator craft were out as the position, early hour and weather were generally unfavourable. However, this afforded the competitors the rare privilege of unobstructed water in which to manoeuvre at the start—unlike Gothenburg in 1978 when there were at least 18,000 densely packed spectator vessels.

Belle Poule and *Etoile*, who always sail in company, passed close by us with other vessels including HMS *Falken* and *Pogoria*. The wind was set fair to blow us through the Baltic Sea, but the morning was overcast, dank and dreary. However, excitement mounted as concentrated action on deck made the crew oblivious to the weather, except when the occasional drip trickled down the neck of an oilskin jacket. Ships' colours were lost in the greyness, sails became as dark shadows. *Kruzenshtern*, with her vast acres of canvas, was levelling up towards the start, with *Guayas* astern, and *Sea Cloud* following. Altogether, there were nine vessels in Class A.

Aboard *Danmark*, Captain Bentsen, peering from beneath his sou'wester, paced the bridge deck, calculating the time before the start. An officer, stop-watch in hand, watched the start boat. The gun fired and a puff of smoke went up from the Danish naval vessel *Lindormen*. Ten minutes to go!

Hidden in the mist astern, waiting backstage to find her cue and gather way behind the rest of the competitors, lay *Sørlandet*. All sails were set now. The ships gained speed in anticipation of the start. The water gurgled past the advancing hulls, waves broke at the bows.

As the final seconds rushed by, eager hands stood by the rigging to trim the sails. Suddenly we were away and first across the line by a bowsprit or two. All nerves were taut as we raced to keep in the lead.

We were pleased with our start. The captain's good judgement had placed us in a favourable position to streak across the line, square-sails set high above our decks. After we set course for Bornholm, the first mark to round, we discussed the start over a typical Scandinavian breakfast: traditional raw herring— invigorating for those strong enough to take it at that early hour—bacon and eggs, cold meats, cheese and jams, accompanied by brown bread, crispy rolls baked by the students, and freshly ground coffee.

The conversation—in Danish intermingled with English—ran on to general speculation about the winner of the 1980 race and then turned to a realisation that it was time to be up on deck again, regular chores seeming all the more interesting by the incentive of competition.

Captain Bentsen had his reclining chair placed on the poop so that he could rest without missing anything by being below. He is a remarkable and convivial character who treats the boys as his own sons, showing consideration to each of them. He began his career at sea in 1936 as a cadet on *Danmark* with Wilhelm Hansen. At that time the First Mate, now called Chief Mate, was Knud Hansen, later to become her Master for many years. They made a long voyage to St Helena, Buenos Aires, Montevideo, the Azores, and then returned to Copen-hagen via Falmouth, where they saw the *Cutty Sark*, lying without sails, but in use as a stationary schoolship. Later that year Bentsen became an ordinary seaman on a three-masted auxiliary schooner trading in fish from Labrador to Exeter. In 1938 he joined powered merchant ships, and, being in England when war was declared, was adopted by the city of Newcastle as his home port during hostilities. He served in the Danish cargo fleet, and, always travelling in convoys, crossed the North Atlantic and went to the Far East. On 13 October 1945, his father's birthday, he returned home. He then studied at navigation school and took his Master's Certificate before rejoining *Danmark* in 1948 as Fifth Officer or Quartermaster. He graduated to Third Officer in 1949, and from 1951 until 1964

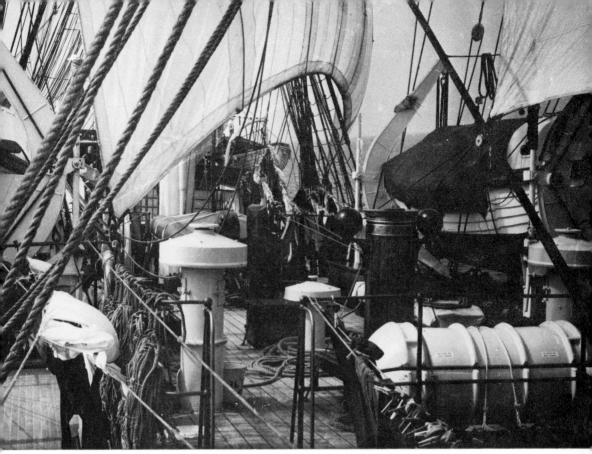

Danmark under sail in Race One, main course sheeted across the boat deck, tack made fast forward to the left of picture, sheets lead aft almost kissing the main port shrouds

sailed as Second Mate under Captain Knud Hansen. Later, he sailed as First Officer to Wilhelm Hansen before becoming Master himself.

TOWARDS BORNHOLM

By 0730 *Dar Pomorza* was ahead of us to port, *Kruzenshtern* was situated close by, almost abeam, with *Gorch Fock* coming up on her far side and *Georg Stage* closely astern of them both. *Sea Cloud*, companion to the fleet but not eligible for a prize, stood well back. *Pogoria* was in sight to port and *Guayas* was moving up from astern.

Positions began to change. By 0800 *Dar Pomorza* was definitely taking the lead, *Gorch Fock*, her close rival, was following hard on her heels, and both were ahead of *Danmark*. Astern of us, near our port quarter, lay *Kruzenshtern* and *Georg Stage*. They were side by side, with *Guayas* rapidly making up ground over them both; she had been astern of us for some time and now began to come forward, heeling finely to the quartering wind. *Sea Cloud* followed her example more gradually, while the progress of *Sørlandet*, our closest rival and counterpart, was being carefully watched from the decks of *Danmark*.

The Russian barque, *Kruzenshtern*, under full sail, preparing for the start of Race One at Falster

Dar Pomorza at the start of the 1976 Tall Ships Race from Plymouth to Tenerife
(Malcolm Darch)

Sørlandet is a little smaller and less heavily built and rigged than *Danmark*, but she had been catching up on us since the start. She had gained speed on our starboard side with seeming ease, rapidly making up for her initial lack of challenge, and showed us her top form although her crew setting all sail were inexperienced. On this second passage her mixed crew of trainees contrasted with *Danmark*'s, whose boys had worked in the rigging for over six months and could climb aloft with the self-assurance of crew who could identify each rope without fumbling, even in the dark. Nevertheless, the trainees on *Sørlandet* were impressive, for, without such intensive training, they had learnt to work on deck and aloft under the instruction of their officers.

We continued the watches and routine chores and paid attention to the sails, the course and accurate navigation, as we headed for the Danish island of Bornholm. Another duty which was done at intervals throughout the six-month voyage was the cleaning of hammocks. Now they had to be prepared for the trainees joining the ship at Frederikshavn. The oblong shapes of canvas were laid out on deck, and, having been thoroughly soaked, were scrubbed, and rinsed. Lines were then strung up on deck for them to dry in the elusive sun, along with the colourful rows of washing which now decorated the foredeck.

AROUND BORNHOLM

At 1800 we were rounding Bornholm and about to alter course for Gotland. The Master talked to the boys lined up on deck—a regular occurrence at change of watch. He explained that the island is famous for the salmon which the local fishermen once caught in profusion around its waters, although stocks are much reduced today. Salmon was one time a staple food for the islanders—mostly fishermen and farmers—but no longer now. Bornholm is also a popular holiday resort with beautiful sandy beaches. The Captain then talked about our course, the weather and conditions, dropping in a joke or amusing story. Our position in the race was reported at regular intervals to keep us alert.

Now it was time for supper, with home-made soup, bread, a hot dish of meat or fish, potatoes and vegetables, followed by coffee and conversation round the table.

The fleet was now running before the wind after rounding Bornholm and we passed *Sea Cloud*, having been level with her all day. We talked with *Georg Stage* as she went close inshore hoping to gain distance. With a south-westerly wind, Force 4–5, we were making 8 knots and could see *Sørlandet*, 3.7 miles ahead on the horizon, as checked on the radar.

SATURDAY 19 JULY

The weather was fair and the wind WSW, Force 4. We were gaining steadily on *Sørlandet*, now ahead by only 2 miles. At 0800 and 0900 the radio schedules commenced transmission, on a prearranged rota. *Somerset*, the guard vessel, called all ships before addressing entrants individually. Some ships' positions were relayed to *Somerset* which steamed through the head of the fleet, leaving *La Vague* posted to cover the rear. This latter motor yacht was chartered to

The German naval barque, *Gorch Fock,* after the 1976 Bermuda to Newport (Rhode Island) Tall Ships Race in foggy conditions

accompany the races to assist communications and administration, by Cornelius Vanderstar, an indomitable Dutchman who now lives in the USA.

Vanderstar began life at sea as a teenager when he set off from his home in Indonesia on a sailing ship, working for some years in the Pacific. Later on, when the island of Java was captured by the Japanese during World War II, he found a yacht and escaped with two companions. They sailed thousands of miles across the Indian Ocean and eventually arrived at the island of Rodriguez. Some years later, after reaching the USA with minimal assets, he set up a prosperous business which has since expanded into Europe. In 1970, at the suggestion of Commander Juta, he sailed aboard *Astral* in the Tall Ships Race from Plymouth to La Coruña. This luxurious bermudan 30-metre (98-foot) LOA centreboard ketch was designed by Philip Rhodes and built by Kroegerwerft at Rendsburg, West Germany in 1970. Vanderstar quickly realised the potential of these events and entered *Astral* as often as possible, scheduling her extensive cruising programme around the races. Sailed either by her owner or her Captain, Dick MacIllvride, an experienced oceanfaring New Zealander, she completed thousands of sea

(*Above*) *Danmark* cadets scrub their hammocks, ready for the next crew; *(below)*
Cadets aboard *Danmark* receiving instruction during Race One

miles' cruising each year. In 1979 Vanderstar donated *Astral* to the United States Naval Academy at Annapolis, which, having refitted her appropriately, participated in the ASTA Race from Boston to Kristiansand in 1980, and then represented the USA at Aalborg in Denmark.

Cornelius Vanderstar appreciates the value of sail training and has assisted many organisations and individuals. He has financed berths aboard the topsail schooners *Sir Winston Churchill* and *Malcolm Miller*, and on the Netherlands Sail Training Association schooner *Eendracht*. He has also endowed a bursary scheme to help youngsters from deprived backgrounds to go to sea on training courses (the allocations are administered by the Association of Sea Training Organisations in Great Britain).

At 0800 we were lying about 12 nautical miles NE of the Ölands Södra Grund Light, 15 miles ENE of the southern tip of Öland, and were now fifth in our class. Ahead of us by about 2 miles lay *Sørlandet*. Beyond her, 18 miles ahead on our starboard bow, lay *Pogoria* in company with the leading ocean racers of Class B III, *Blanca Estela* and *Queen*. *Dar Pomorza* was ahead of us by 11 miles and *Guayas* by 6.5 miles. *Gorch Fock*, placed fourth in her class on corrected time, lay 10 miles ahead of us, further to starboard. Astern of us lay *Georg Stage*, about 6 miles back and first in corrected position, and *Sea Cloud*. She was near *Kruzenshtern* which was third, while *Creole* was further aft by a few miles. The tail of the fleet was 90 miles behind *Danmark*, with *Jens Krogh*, the 58 Thames tons Danish gaff ketch, in the rear. Later on we began to gain on *Sørlandet*. The wind was WSW, Force 4, as we headed for Gotland.

RADIO COMMUNICATIONS

Radio links throughout the races were the prime aid to safety and the implementing of emergency procedures that are essential to a fleet of such proportions. There was also instant help between competitors, which was often evident and usually went unrecorded. For instance, on the evening of Saturday 19 July a boy on board *Urania* was suffering from severe toothache. A message was relayed to *Somerset* who plotted *Urania*'s position and had the boy transported ashore for treatment at the port of Visby on the west coast of Gotland.

On Sunday 20 July a girl trainee aboard the yacht *Cereola* seriously injured a finger in a winch accident. Through contact with *Somerset* and HMS *Falken*, swift relief came when the Royal Swedish Navy transported her by helicopter to a hospital on Gotland.

The Skipper of *Ramrod* was taken ashore by *Somerset* to Slite on the east coast of Gotland to get medical attention for an infected throat. He then rejoined the yacht, which is owned by the Colchester Divisional Scout Sail Training Scheme and crewed by members of the Scouts, Rangers, and other youth organisations. *Ramrod*, an auxiliary mast-head cutter, was designed by Arthur Robb and built of double teak planking in 1959 by Port Hamble Limited. She has a distinguished record as an ocean racer, including a successful challenge in the Admirals Cup Team of 1959. She is based at West Mersea on the east coast of England.

Messages of a more social nature were also relayed between ships. For instance,

Danmark: the set of the sails, note the view, looking directly up the mast, which is hidden behind the sails, and the gradual curve of the sails, produced by the yards being positioned in a slight spiral, to gain most effect from the wind

Limp sails on *Danmark* during the calm in Race One

when TS *Royalist* and *Eendracht* were sailing close together, the former offered to tow astern a bottle of spirit for the Dutch schooner to pick up as she was passed. *Eendracht*, however, had no intention of being overtaken, was not going to contemplate the possibility, and replied that she would tow some suitable Dutch spirit in her wake for the British brig to retrieve, as compensation for remaining astern!

As the course narrowed between Gotland and the Swedish coast there were often scores of vessels still within sight of one another and this proximity enhanced interest, for it was exciting to see one's close rivals.

Over the radio, competitors became familiar with 'Madame Butterfly' from the American schooner *Le Papillon*, aptly named by Chris Phelan when Morin Scott had temporarily monopolised the attractive voice on the air, by trying to discover from which American state the lady came. *Royalist* actually held a lottery on the origin of this accent which had so fascinated its crew. Apparently, the voice of Tom Lemm, owner of *Le Papillon*, did not attract the same interest as Donna Lynn's!

APPROACHING GOTLAND

Onshore lights came into view as we neared the northern coast of Gotland on 20 July. We sailed slowly by, square-sails set high above our decks. At 0300 we were about 7 miles off Visby, an ancient Hanseatic port on the west coast of Gotland. We were making 3.8 knots and approaching the coastline on a NNE course. The duty watch, standing in the open fo'c'sle, waited for orders to call them to work.

It was a bright dawn and to our starboard side *Eendracht* passed ahead of us through the calm seas. At 0758 the crew were on deck awaiting the Captain's situation report. After breakfast, I watched him admiring the set of the sails, skilfully judging the trim like an artist studying the composition of a painting.

Gratitude of Gothenburg was close by, her red mizzen staysail set between the masts. *Gratia of Gothenburg* passed us with sails billowing in the light breeze. Over the radio we remarked how good it was to see her, but wondered whether it was not a mistake to overtake us, as she had made the same tactical error the day before. She was sure, however, that it was a good move this time, and had calculated the benefits of passing us. This brief conversation resulted in mutual invitations for visits in Karlskrona.

The bermudan ketch *Halcyon* could be heard talking to *Hoshi* over the radio. Built in 1929 at the Woolston Yard of John Thornycroft & Company of Southampton, *Halcyon* is 30 metres (98 feet) LOA, 53 gross tons and 78 Thames tons. Owned by Hampshire County Council, she is sailed and administered by the College of Nautical Studies at Warsash, Southampton, which also owns *Somerset*. Since 1956, when she was purchased to replace *Moyana*, winner of the first Tall Ships Race, she has maintained the tradition of sail training for Merchant Navy cadets. She is also available for schools, colleges and youth organisations. In 1980 her Master was Captain J. H. Kennedy and she sailed with trainees from the BP Company which had chartered the berths for the duration of these races.

Hard at work polishing the brass binnacle during Race One on *Danmark*

Later we heard *Sparta* from the USSR, a bermudan sloop launched in Poland in 1980. She is owned by the Latvian Shipping Company, and sailed with four officers and six pupils of the Riga Nautical School. The cadets were all novices who, before the races, spent a month in part-time training, their studies including sport and English. Her Master, Captain Alexander Chechulin, instructs at the Leningrad Marine Engineering College, and sailed on board the Russian barque *Tovarisch* (ex-*Gorch Fock I*) in the 1976 series of Tall Ships Races across the Atlantic to the United States. He skippered the sloop *Ritza*, the first Russian yacht to enter the races, in the 1978 event from Gothenburg to Oslo via Fair Isle, when she was placed second in her class. One of the smallest competitors, she was entered in 1980 with cadets from the Leningrad Marine Engineering College, which owns her, under Captain Antonov who was her Chief Mate in 1978.

The positions of the ships were being relayed over the radio again. *Dar Pomorza* lay 8 miles NW of the Fårö Light, situated on the northern extremity of Fårö Island off the north-east coast of Gotland, *Gorch Fock* was only $2\frac{1}{2}$ miles astern of her, and to port of these two vessels lay HMS *Falken*, which was 2 miles ahead of *Donald Searle*. *Guayas* lay close astern of them all with *Pogoria* a short way ahead. The Class B III leaders, *Queen* and *Blanca Estela*, were respectively 20 miles due south and 22 miles just east of south from the Fårö Light.

The gaff cutter,
Olifant von Wedel,
the 36-foot mini-
entrant from West
Germany
(Heinrich Woermann)

Aloft on TS *Royalist*: the Bosun instructs sea cadets to stow and furl the fore-topsail,
while others work on the main yards *(The Sea Cadet Corps)*

We lay to the west on the opposite side of the island. Our position was about 44 miles astern of *Dar Pomorza*; behind us, 4 miles away, was *Kruzenshtern*; *Creole*, 7 miles and *Georg Stage*, 14 miles behind. Further astern was *Jolie Brise*, classic yacht of the twenties and winner of the first Fastnet Race, who is now owned by the Exeter Maritime Museum and sailed by Dauntsey's School. *Olifant von Wedel*, the mini-entrant from West Germany, was over 30 miles away. This 11-metre (36-foot) LOA black gaff cutter was built for her owner Heinrich Woermann in 1977. She was designed by Skibsbygmester Michael Kiersgaard in Troense near Svendborg on the lines of the typical Danish or Baltic *jagt*—a fast coastal cargo vessel sailed in these waters. She was constructed at Marstal in Denmark from traditional materials—larch-wood planks on oak keel and ribs— and is rigged in the traditional way, including a square-sail for running before the wind. This charming craft carries a maximum crew of five, and although she does not participate officially in sail training, her owner invited young people to join him under sail—to the enhancement of the STA Race.

Another gaffer of Class B I, *Dusmarie*, lying about 45 miles behind us, was familiar to regular competitors of the races. She is a converted oyster-smack built in 1884, 13-metres (43¾-foot) LOA, 16 Thames tons, and owned by Mary Dixon and her daughter Astrid Westbury who skippered her in 1980. Having been used for fifty years as a working smack called *Daisy*, she was bought in 1933 by the late Lieutenant-Commander Douglas Dixon and his wife Mary as a cruising home. She has remained in the family for nearly fifty years under the name of *Dusmarie*. In 1933 she won third prize in the Channel Race, in 1937–8 she sailed to the Gulf of Bothnia, in 1946 she was redesigned from cutter to yawl rig and rebuilt in Sweden. From 1947 to 1956 she became the flagship of the Manno expedition flotilla for schoolboys, and cruised with them in Holland and on the west coast of Sweden. Between 1957 and 1959 she sailed to Gallipoli, the years in which Mrs Dixon founded Branson's College with the support of her husband. Its aims are to strengthen young people's interest in the Commonwealth and to develop self-discipline, personal responsibility and enjoy the freedom of the open sea and country. The college is in Suffolk, and in 1967 opened a branch in Quebec province. Courses provide a wide range of A-level subjects, travel, cultural and sporting activities, which in England since 1964 have included sail training aboard *Dusmarie* during the summer months, usually on cruises to the Baltic.

Dusmarie entered the Tall Ships Races for the first time in 1974 with an all-female crew, from Copenhagen to Gdynia. She has since raced on various STA occasions with either girls, boys or a mixed crew, under her Skipper Astrid Westbury.

TACKING NORTH OF GOTLAND
We continued along the north-western coast of Gotland, eager to round this mark. However, the adverse wind forced us to tack around the north of the island.

At 1425 we were about 13 miles due north of the Fårö Lighthouse. At 1527 our position was 16 miles NNE of the light, and we were making 4½ knots on a

course of o6o degrees true. We tacked ship. I manned the forecourse tack on the
fo'c'sle, listening to the orders from the Bosun. Once all was prepared the action
began: every rope had to be ready and free to run, before we could start.

> *Everything is now ready, and it* must *be ready—no oversights, no stupidity. The whole success
> of the manoeuvre rests on foresight and organisation beforehand, as in so much of the square-
> rigger's work.*

ALAN VILLIERS, The Way of a Ship

The boys stood by their stations, awaiting orders as the ship was eased off the
wind to build up maximum speed to help her turn through the eye of the wind.
Lee braces were flaked out on deck, clear to run, and spanker brought amidships.
Then, as the wheel was put right over, the 'tween mast staysails were dropped
out of the way. The courses were raised up about two-thirds from the deck to
clear the ship's boats; the yards on the main and mizzen masts spun round as the
orders were given. It was essential for the timing of this operation to be just right
so that the ship would not loose way. She was turning, with the jibs, staysails and
sails on the foremast aback to help push the bows round; the decks were already a
maze of ropes. Sails on the main and mizzen masts began to fill again: then the
foremast was braced round, jibs and staysails sheeted home, 'tween mast staysails
reset, fore and main courses set into action again, tack of the forecourse brought
well home with the aid of the capstan, course steadied and the spanker eased off as
necessary.

In the mist we could see fellow competitors also trying to make headway in
the frustratingly difficult conditions. Some vessels were carried well to the north,
while others chose to stay inshore. *Gratitude*, under the experienced command of
Kjell Wollter, crept towards the coast on each tack. With no modern devices to
sound the depth or scan the lie of the land, his crew depended on the leadline: one
of the trainees would heave out the long leadline and anxiously look at the
marks.

By 1723 the wind had changed a little and pushed us further north. We tacked
again on to a course heading almost due south, until at 2000 we were about 6
miles north-east of the Fårö Lighthouse. We sailed a course just south of east for
about 10 miles and we then made about 15 miles in a south-easterly direction
during the four hours before midnight, when it was time for the change of
watch.

We were still on a south-easterly course 4 hours and 16 miles later. Watch
duties continued. Two boys usually took the wheel for one-hour tricks. Look-

Dusmarie (sail number 822) seen racing on the east coast of England. She participated
in the Tall Ships Races in 1980 with a crew from Bransons Commonwealth
Educational Trust, skippered by Astrid Westbury (*Astrid Westbury*)

(Left) Albatros, three-masted gaff schooner owned by Clipper, Deutsches Jugendwerk zur
See eV; *(right)* aloft on the fore-yard, trainees from Mariners International aboard the
gaff schooner *El Pirata* owned by John Cluett of Guernsey. Crowds line the banks for
the Parade of Sail at Bremerhaven, August 1980 (*Stadtbildstelle Seestadt Bremerhaven*)

Captain Chris Phelan, Master of *Somerset*, during the Cutty Sark Tall Ships Races. He is Director of the College of Nautical Studies at Warsash. *Halcyon*, which trains cadets from the College, alongside. *Creole* in distance on right *(D. J. Benstead)*

outs were posted on port and starboard on the bridge deck and another forward in the bows. Bells were sounded to indicate lights—one for starboard, two for port, and three ahead. The navigator studied the course while an officer checked the radar. As another competitor tacked close across our stern, the watch realised the necessity for great vigilance in case of approaching danger in the poor visibility.

MONDAY 21 JULY

At 1200 *Somerset* reported the current positions: *Sørlandet* had taken a diversion, to our benefit, and was now 25 miles astern of us, north-east, and was heading towards Russia en route for the Bay of Riga. *Kruzenshtern* was 22 miles and *Georg Stage* 25 miles astern of us, about 10 and 12 miles north-west of the Fårö Light. *Le Papillon*, *Anna Rosa* and *Seute Deern* were over 30 miles away to the north of the light. *El Pirata*, entered by Mariners International which had chartered her from John Cluett who was Master during the voyage, was even further north. She eventually retired, head winds having defeated her chances.

Ahead of *Danmark* by 33 miles lay *Gorch Fock*, situated 10 miles north-east of the Östergarn Light; *Dar Pomorza* was 10 miles due east of her. Further on, *Belle Poule*, the French naval topsail schooner, was 16 miles beyond her sister ship *Etoile*.

Georg Stage, Danish full-rigged ship, under sail *(Captain B. Barner Jespersen and the Georg Stages Minde)*

Cadets on *Georg Stage* studying in the mess deck. Lessons go on throughout cruises and races *(Captain B. Barner Jespersen, Georg Stages Minde)*

These twins, built in 1932 for the French Naval Academy, spend 260 days each year training cadets on short courses based from the naval port of Brest.

About 16 miles ahead of the leading French schooner *Belle Poule* lay *Pogoria*, and ahead of her was the Bavarian crewed *Isis*. *Guayas* lay further to the south-east of these, but behind the speedy spinnaker set which included *Hetman*, *Urania*, *Avalanche*, *Hajduk*, *Ritza*, *Flamingo* and *Walross III*. At least 40 miles south-west of the southern tip of Gotland, leading the fleet, were *Wojewoda Pomorski*, *Queen* and *Blanca Estela*. On corrected time we were fourth in our class, a pleasing result at that stage: the situation had changed to our advantage and we hoped to maintain or even improve this during the next days.

GEORG STAGE

The First and Second Officers of *Danmark*, Ole Ingrisch and Steffen Schultz, had both sailed together aboard the full-rigged ship *Georg Stage*, first as cadets, then more recently as Mates. They described her background to me in some detail.

The Georg Stage Memorial Foundation was established and endowed in 1882 by Carl Frederik Stage, a Danish ship-owner, and his wife Thea, in memory of their son Georg who had died when he was 22 years old. The purpose of the foundation was, and still is, to give boys who aim to enter the Merchant Navy a sound grounding in practical seamanship. Great importance is attached to preparatory training on board before passages are made throughout the Baltic and North Seas.

The three-masted gaff schooner *Elinor*: examining the damage she sustained from a fishing boat at the end of Race One *(D. J. Benstead)*

The Georg Stages Minde is controlled by a Board of Governors, who are usually connected with shipping or with the Royal Danish Navy, and always includes a member of the Stage family. Funds for the ship come from the original trust of C. F. Stage, private contributions, friends of *Georg Stage* and the Danish Government.

Georg Stage was built in 1882 at the Burmeister and Wain Yard in Copenhagen as a full-rigged ship of iron, with a registered length of 31 metres (101 feet) and 203 registered gross tons. An auxiliary steam engine was fitted but was mere ballast as it was seldom used. She carried single topsails and her rigging was set up with dead-eyes and lanyards to outside channels. She sailed every year from 1882 to 1934 with only three exceptions. Eighty boys aged from 15 to 18 years sailed on board for five months each summer. In winter she was laid up and her gear taken ashore, examined and overhauled for the following season.

In the early 1930s the *Georg Stage* was growing old and, with the help of the Danish Government and other support, a vessel was commissioned to replace her. She was to retain the original name, but be of modern design and slightly larger, able to carry ten officers and sixty cadets. This new ship was constructed at the yard of Vaerft and Flydedok A/S of Frederikshavn, Denmark. She is a three-masted, full-rigged ship of 298 gross tons, and 46 metres (151 feet) length overall, with a sail area of 859 square metres, including double topsails. She is fitted with an auxiliary diesel engine.

JOSEPH CONRAD, ex-GEORG STAGE

In 1934, when *Georg Stage* was about to be retired from service in Denmark, Alan Villiers saw her manoeuvring under sail in Copenhagen Harbour. He was so impressed that he purchased her and, when she had completed her training programme that summer, he sailed her to England and refitted her at Ipswich. Her name was changed to *Joseph Conrad* and a round-the-world voyage was planned for a crew of boys under the guidance of an experienced afterguard. The intention was to introduce the young cadets to a way of life afloat rather than to train them specifically for a career—a novel idea at that time. There were to be classes on seamanship, as well as practical deck work and watch-keeping routines. The boys who could afford to pay contributed towards the expense of the voyage; apart from the Captain's funds, there were no other subsidies. Alan Villiers was Master and the professional crew, most of whom were in their early twenties, consisted of three mates, bosun, carpenter, sail-maker, cook, steward and three ABs. Many of them had gained experience sailing in the Baltic trade or on grain ships to Australia. The whole complement was international, including Australians, Danes, Finns, English, Germans, Americans, South Africans and New Zealanders.

From October 1934 to October 1936 the ship sailed 57,800 nautical miles around the world, rounding Cape Horn and visiting many places en route. It was a memorable voyage and Villiers recorded its details in his volume of photographs entitled *The Making of a Sailor*, and in *The Cruise of the Conrad*.

As Villiers received no financial backing he was forced to sell her at the end of the voyage in New York. The millionaire baker Huntington Hartford bought her for conversion to a private yacht, and she sailed for a year or two before he gave her to the United States Maritime Commission as a training ship for the cadets of the merchant service. Between 1939 and 1945 she was based at St Petersburg, Florida, from where she cruised, before she became a stationary schoolship. In 1947 she was presented to the Marine Historical Association Incorporated, and was towed to Mystic Seaport in Connecticut, USA, where she can be seen today.

DANMARK'S CREW

On board *Danmark* I learnt of the many places her officers had visited. For instance, the First Mate had worked in Greenland for one and half years on the Fisheries Protection Service—a tough job during the dark, frozen winter months. Later he had sailed to Africa and the Far East. And Knud Vang Nielsen, Chief Mate for the race, had worked on the Amazon and travelled up river to Manaus—quite different from the open seas of the Atlantic and Pacific Oceans.

BECALMED

One evening, *Svanen of Stockholm* and *Hoshi* lay becalmed on the motionless sea at twilight—that long, clear, lingering light of northern waters in summer. Reaching close together, they tied up alongside for a barbecue, set up on *Svanen's* steel decks and organised by her Skipper, the tall Swede, Carl Magnus Ring. He had purchased *Svanen* four years earlier to convert her from a steamer to a sailing

Cadets scrubbing the decks aboard *Danmark*

staysail schooner. He did most of the work himself while living in Stockholm and now sails with a crew from mixed backgrounds, usually including two boys sponsored by the Swedish Government as a means of social work. Cod caught by the ships' crews amply supplied the fire to feed the hungry appetites aboard, and, as no breeze sprang up, the party continued into the long cool evening.

THE FINISHING LINE
No official position reportings were given on 22 July as some of the fleet had already arrived at Karlskrona. *Somerset* was there and was setting up the Race Office.

Blanca Estela arrived first followed by *Queen, Walross III, Sabre* and other swift rivals. At midday we lay 5 miles south-east of the Ölands Södra Udde Light which marks the southern tip of Öland. We had to sail just over 30 miles before reaching the line which ran due south from the Utklippan Lighthouse for 12 miles. Astern of us we could see *Royalist*, then *Kruzenshtern, Sørlandet* and, on the horizon, *Georg Stage*. We sailed slowly on through the still sea, knowing that the fastest rivals of our class, *Pogoria, Dar Pomorza, Gorch Fock* and *Guayas*, had already made the line! Later that afternoon, *Donald Searle* finished the race very close to *Falken*, and, before entering harbour, both anchored nearby the line where they conversed and enjoyed the final stages of the race for other competitors, including a most spectacular finale for the French schooners, with *Etoile* clipping the line less than a bowsprit ahead of her sister ship *Belle Poule*.

That evening, as *Danmark* neared the finishing line with only a whisper of a breeze to push her onwards, we witnessed a remarkable eclipse of the sun. Silhouetted against the sunset sky, the Danish schooner *Elinor*, her three-masted gaff rig laden with sails, floated across the fiery path of the sun. The silence was disturbed by the clicking of cameras as the decks were lined by avid photographers. I was so moved to be undecided whether to simply stand and stare and drink in the atmosphere or to record its peaceful splendour. I captured the scene on film, however—a decision I have not regretted.

Later, at 0300, when *Danmark* had just crossed the line, we were distressed to hear a Mayday call: *Elinor* had been hit by a fishing boat. Needlessly rammed, she lay severely damaged, the planking from her starboard quarter torn away and crushed down to the waterline, her boat and davits wrenched from under her. The sleepy fisherman, unwary of the possibility of collision, had simply slipped away from the scene.

We turned to go and stand by her, for she was taking in water. Her pumps, although fully manned, could hardly cope at first; most of the crew were in a state of shock and one member had an injured arm. Before we arrived on the scene, *Royalist*, who was still in the race, altered course to pick up wreckage, the ship's boat, and to stand by. However, *Elinor* was able to limp slowly into harbour without assistance. It was a great blow for this fine ship which would require time, expense and skill to repair. At the prize-giving in Karlskrona she was given a special award as some consolation for this avoidable misadventure which wrecked her summer cruising and caused her to withdraw from Race Two.

Danmark lying outside *Gorch Fock* at the commercial dock, Karlskrona *(Lt Col Roger Cemm)*

6

KARLSKRONA

The real delight of the Tall Ships Races is that every participant comes to understand that it is more important to take part than to win.

LIEUTENANT-COLONEL, THE LORD BURNHAM, JP, CHAIRMAN OF THE SAIL TRAINING ASSOCI-
ATION, STA *Race Programme* (1978)

On a sunny morning we passed through the narrow band of lush islands which guard Karlskrona Harbour and make it almost impregnable. Until 1658 this southern region of Sweden, Blekinge, was in the hands of the Danes but in 1680 Karlskrona was founded by Charles XI of Sweden because its situation made it an excellent naval base. The three hundredth anniversary of the town's foundation was celebrated in 1980 and among its festivities was the welcoming of the tall ships after the race from Kiel.

Stortorget Square, which is surrounded by large Baroque buildings, dominates the town from its hill-top position. Wide tree-lined streets lead from it past the shopping area to attractive parks or to the sea which surrounds the town on three sides. Open-air cafés, market, flags, flowers, nearby beaches and islands make it a popular holiday resort.

Karlskrona's livelihood is dependent on the Royal Swedish Navy, and is still an important centre for the naval base. Many historical features are retained at the base, including the rope-walk built in 1691–6, which, at over 300 metres (984 feet), is the longest wooden building in Sweden. The mast crane is a significant landmark. Johan Tornstrom's eighteenth-century workshop is famous for his carved figureheads, many of which are on display at the Maritime Museum where local naval and nautical history are given special attention.

The cadets on board *Gorch Fock* which had moored the previous day, having missed the calm which left us frustratingly at sea, watched as we came alongside them. *Danmark*'s boat was lowered from the port quarter and we jostled into position beside the German barque while carefully observing the yards above. We made fast, the gangways were lowered and soon friends were exchanging greetings as the city officials arrived on board. The Mayor, accompanied by Commodore Ahrén, Chairman of the Karlskrona Committee, Torsten Wikström, the Town Clerk, and Sonnie Nilsson addressed the Captain and cordially welcomed the ship— the first example of the hospitality and organisation which the Swedes were to show throughout our stay.

We then enjoyed a traditional Danish luncheon of *smørrebrød*, with schnapps, hot dishes, cheese and coffee. Informal discussions with the Liaison Officer related the programme of events and the Stores Liaison Officer was consulted by the Chief Steward about revictualling the ship. The cadets were to enjoy bus tours of the city, visits to the Warmopark, dancing in the evening, free transport through a badge identification system, beach parties, a barbecue and entertainments. A telephone service, 'Dial-a-sailor', gave locals the opportunity to take cadets into their own homes and show them the Swedish way of life for a few hours. Maps and other information were issued to everyone, while the Captain received an outline of official calls. Naval officers provided this link for the entire fleet—clear communications being essential for the running of large-scale shore activities. Two of the officers in charge of this operation were Commander Sten Gattberg, a past participant in the races, including the series to the USA aboard HMS *Gladan* in 1976, and Lieutenant-Commander Claes Öquist who had also entered these events on Swedish naval training schooners, most memorably in 1978 when *Gladan* was awarded the Cutty Sark Trophy for International Friendship and Understanding.

The off-duty cadets on *Danmark* were designated leave to be taken in turns, as one watch was required to stay on board. Class A vessels were berthed at the commercial harbour; we lay outside *Gorch Fock* with *Dar Pomorza*, first in our class, astern. Beyond her, *Sørlandet* would berth on arrival, while *Guayas*, second in class, and our non-racing companion *Sea Cloud*, were already alongside. *Georg Stage*, *Creole* and *Kruzenshtern* were yet to come.

A Liaison Officer drove me to the naval harbour, about 1.6 kilometres (1 mile) away, where the remainder of the fleet which had already finished were docked. These included many of the Class B vessels as well as *Pogoria* from Class A and *Somerset*. Walking along the quayside, I met among other people Captain Tadeusz Olechnowicz, Master of *Dar Pomorza*, who was enjoying the opportunity to relax.

Walross III's crew were inviting guests to join them for a barbecue, while others were busy aboard their own vessels. The miniature tender to *Olifant* lay alongside her. There was *Chwan*, the local bermudan ketch, and *Urania*, *Wojewoda Pomorski*, *Ellida* and *Roztocze*. *Isis*, a West German bermudan ketch, *Medea*, a Swiss bermudan sloop, and the classic West German sloop *Athena*, had been chartered by crews from Bavaria who had been eager to join the events for the past eight years. They donated three prizes which they gave to the STA on *Somerset* at Karlskrona. These were presented at the end of Race Two in Amsterdam, and included a traditional Bavarian cow-bell. I also saw *Dark Horse*, a modern white schooner owned by Lloyd's Bank, whose crew appeared in matching red guernseys embroidered with the ship's name. She takes bank employees to sea in the summer as well as participating in the races.

Some of the vessels had sailed in company for much of the race, and a few hours after *Danmark* had crossed the line, *Dione*, *Hoshi*, *Sørlandet*, *Equinoxe*, *Carola*, *Georg Stage* and *Svanen of Stockholm* finished within a short time of each other. *Equinoxe* was built as a Bristol Channel pilot cutter in 1913 at the same yard as *Belle Poule* and *Etoile*. Later, she was converted as a yacht, and in the 1960s was

Daniel Moreland, *Danmark*'s American Bosun admiring the square-riggers at
Karlskrona: *Sørlandet* on the right, ahead of her *Dar Pomorza*, and outside her *Creole*

Class B vessels at the naval harbour at Karlskrona; *Roztocze*'s red and white Polish flag in front of *British Soldier*

used for training by the Ocean Youth Club. Since 1975 her German owner had been restoring her above and below decks, so that she was sound for his first major voyage. *Urania, Carola, Peter von Danzig, Blanca Estela* and *Cereola*, the comfortable white bermudan ketch owned by Greville Howard and skippered by Sonny Evans, were among the many vessels now in harbour.

Meanwhile, intership rivalry among the British Kiel Yacht Club yachts had resulted in *Kranich* finishing behind *Avalanche* but ahead of *Flamingo*. The gunner yacht *St Barbara II* had also raced from her base at Kiel. The Royal Artillery are keen supporters of the races and had also supplied a crew for HMSTY *British Soldier*, one of the Nicholson 55s owned by the Joint Services Sailing Centre at Gosport. This vessel had retired from Race One after blowing out a spinnaker and other sails, and damaging a mast track while en route to the start. After returning to Kiel for repairs, she had cruised to Karlskrona enjoying the scenery on the way. HMSTY *Dasher*, her sister ship, entered by the Royal Navy, had also retired for similar reasons, while HMSTY *Sabre* had come in fourth over the line.

The Joint Services Sailing Centre allocates these yachts between the three services. At sea, all servicemen are treated alike, and the NCO can skipper a yacht on which a general may be the deck hand or an admiral may be under the command of a petty officer. The scheme also encourages all servicemen to take part in sporting activities, thereby using their leisure time constructively. The training aims towards the RYA/DTI Yachtmaster Certificate. The cost of these yachts, plus others at the centre, is paid for by the British Government. No civilians participate in the courses, apart from the instructors. The centre also owns numerous smaller cruising yachts, and nine Nicholson 55s which have accumulated thousands of miles of sail training. *Adventure*, for instance, has raced twice around the world with a Royal Navy crew which changed at the end of each leg to enable the maximum number of trainees to participate. In 1979 alone, berths were available for 4,696 trainees for an average of a week. The yachts operate from March to November, except for the vessels which sail farther south to tropical seas for the winter.

The Danish schooner *Elinor* now lay distressed by the quay, her whole starboard quarter torn away to the waterline. As skills in wood and the materials are not always readily available, and as the repair work would be time-consuming, it was decided to move her across to a yard in Denmark on a calm day as any lop would break over her exposed hull. Her unfortunate owners tried to piece together the wreckage, some of which had been picked up by TS *Royalist*.

Aboard the brig I was almost persuaded to join the 92 Thames tons gaff schooner *Atene* for a mini-cruise to Christiansø, a remote islet off Bornholm, but I was reluctant to leave the activity for any length of time. The crew of *Atene* were Danish, although the ship was registered in Sweden, and sadly had suffered the loss of her owner, Einar Karlsson, who had died suddenly at Kiel. The crew had decided to continue the race under the command of Jens Norregaard.

General view of Class B ships at the naval base at Karlskrona: HMSTY *Sabre* left foreground, crewed by the REME

Lord Burnham, Chairman of the
Sail Training Association, with
Janka Bielak, 'Madame STA'
(who took some of the photographs
in this book), at Oslo in 1978
(Henryk Kabat)

The trainees had come from various yacht clubs around Denmark and were
familiar with dinghy sailing but new to larger vessels. Both they and the officers,
who were also new to the STA circuit, found it a worthwhile and valuable
experience. The Captain found the STA's interest in the young people and the
internationality very rewarding, and was struck by the first question he was
asked when returning his declaration form after the race: 'How did the boys like
it?'—a consideration of paramount importance throughout the events.

A NEW ARRIVAL
As I walked along the quay to congratulate the crew of HMS *Falken* for being first
in her class, I saw an official car driving slowly through the crowds. Inside, were
Greville Howard, his wife Mary, and Mrs Janka Bielak, 'Madame STA', who
were on their way to greet a new arrival who was joining them. Mrs Bielak, one
of the stalwart volunteers on these occasions, is an understanding and helpful
Polish interpreter who aids the success of internationality. She is also an enthusiastic sailor, having manned the yards on the STA schooners and been a great
support to her Skipper, Charlie Gladdis, on board *Carillion of Wight* in 1979 for
the Lancia Tall Ships Race to the Isle of Man when she was one of the few to
withstand the gale.

Malcolm Miller:
(top) girl trainee steering following instructions from watch officer; *(centre and bottom)*
girls stowing sails *(Janka Bielak)*

As I approached HMS *Falken* the flags were already set below the awning and I was welcomed aboard by the captain, Ragnar Westblad. Swedish hospitality flowed freely during the celebratory evening and the crew congratulated their captain by throwing him overboard.

CLIPPER

The German organisation Clipper was founded in 1973 by a small group of enthusiasts and experienced sailors for training youth at sea. Influenced by the Windjammer Parade of 1972 at Kiel, the retired naval Captain Hans Engel, who had for many years been in command of the training barque *Gorch Fock*, engendered the idea and produced the initial plans for Clipper Deutsches Jugendwerk zur See eV, which is run by a council. All the officers, cooks, engineers, qualified crew and secretaries are volunteers, who usually contribute cash as well as time. Only in this way can the ships run on a low budget, which the organisation tries to maintain. During the summer, the two-week courses are generally based at Travemünde and sail in the Baltic Sea.

Seute Deern, the 36-metre (118-foot) LOA black ketch was built as *Havet* in 1936 at Ring Andersen's Shipyard, Svendborg, for the Danish Government. She was used for geophysical research in the South Pacific 1936–7. During World War II she was laid up and then sold to J. Lauritzen for training under the name *Noona Dan*. In 1964 she was bought by the Deutscher Schulschiffverein Oldenburg and the Stiftung Pamir-Passat, which have chartered her to Clipper since 1973. Her

A distinguished section of the brass band from *Guayas*, giving a concert on *Danmark* at Karlskrona

Captain in 1980 for Race One was Peter Lohmeyer who has been involved with Clipper from the beginning.

Amphitrite joined the fleet in late 1973. Built in 1887 by Camper and Nicholson's, she was launched as a two-masted gaff schooner. From about 1947 she was owned by Colonel Charters who kept her at Salcombe in South Devon. In 1956 she was sold and rerigged as a three-masted schooner and set off towards the Mediterranean where she had problems with gun-running. Later, as a barquentine, she was used for filming, until Clipper found her at the end of 1973. She joined the fleet and was rerigged as a three-masted gaff schooner.

Albatros, which was built as a Baltic trader at Hobro, Denmark, in 1942, was renamed by Clipper in 1978 when she was bought from Tony Davies of Brightlingsea. He had spent some years restoring her as the three-masted topsail schooner which was used in the *Onedin Line* television series.

Nearby, the Skipper of the gaff ketch *Gratitude of Gothenburg* had summoned three of the hard-working official organisers to visit his vessel at 1100 that morning. They were greeted on deck, and when all had assembled, both Commodore Ahrén, Chairman of the Karlskrona Committee, and John Hamilton were presented with mobiles of models of the three Swedish Cruising Association ketches. They were delightfully surprised by this show of appreciation, but rather dismayed by the apparent dismissal of the other guest, the King's Harbour Master, Commander Thor Widell. However, the next moment Kjell Wollter struck a resounding note on the ship's bell and in the same movement presented Captain Widell with the decorative rope which had appeared until then to be hanging securely beneath the bell.

A CONCERT ON *DANMARK*

A live radio concert was broadcast from *Danmark* with participants from the tall ships. Everyone assembled on the decks where they were surrounded by cables, wires, microphones, assistants and producers. On the foredeck and main deck areas were set aside for recording. After a rehearsal period the concert was broadcast: music was performed by the crews of *Belle Poule* and *Etoile*; there were songs from *Gratia* and *Gratitude*; Polish tunes played by guitarists from *Dar Pomorza*; a musical offering from *Danmark*, and the familiar brass band of *Guayas*.

Greville Howard gave a short speech, and the crew of *Somerset* sang heartily. Then modern Russian melodies and further musical entertainment were performed.

The concert was also heard at the beach parties given by Karlskrona City Council and Naval Base South, which were held on two consecutive nights for cadets and crews. A pop group played at the parties as well as the ships' own musicians, whose standard of musicianship was outstanding. Among other performers was the mouth-organist from *Symfoni*, a Dutch charter yacht, and the *Grønland* shanty crew accompanied by the accordion playing of Günther Bockelmann.

SUNSET

Along the quay, above the many different hulls constructed of steel, wood or glass-fibre composites, arose a forest of masts. All were decorated by the cordage of sailing: miles of standing and running rigging, and wires and ropes composing halliards, sheets, foot-ropes, ratlines, falls, tackles, shrouds, stays, baggywrinkle and braces. Neatly stowed sails lay along booms and yards. The ships were dressed during the day with colourful flags which fluttered from mast-heads to waterlines. At the official recognition of sunset the most senior vessel or station would lower its flags, and all vessels would follow suit. This operation was an impressive co-ordination viewed from the square-riggers or their smaller counterparts, where the cadets would stand near the appropriate ensign and flag halliards, pipes would sound, all hands would face aft and officers on the ships would salute.

John Marriner, owner of *Morning Watch*, the motor-powered companion to the races, was attentively watching the ceremony. He is an author whose cruising experiences aboard *Morning Watch* and her predecessors, *September Tide* and *Dame des Iles*, have covered thousands of miles of coastlines, rivers and inland waterways. He has travelled particularly throughout Europe, including the Mediterranean and Baltic Seas, voyaging along the Danube and behind the Iron Curtain, and his was the first private vessel to visit Poland after World War II. In 1980 he returned from the United States via Bermuda and the Azores, joining these ships in Kiel to act as a communication guard ship and base for officials, thereby helping the administration. In Karlskrona his hospitality was appreciated by Lord Burnham, who is a keen sailor himself and has, since he retired from the Scots Guards, taken a great interest in the race organisation and sail training for youth in Britain, particularly as the Chairman of the STA.

LIEUTENANT-COLONEL JAMES MYATT AND SAIL TRAINING

James Myatt, a member of the STA Sailing Committee, has participated in many of the races since the early sixties when he persuaded the Royal Artillery Yacht Club to enter their sloop *St Barbara* in the STA event from Torbay to Rotterdam. In 1964 he advanced interest in the prospect of building a training ship for Britain when he organised an entry to represent the country and the STA for two races—the first from Plymouth to Lisbon, and the second across the Atlantic to Bermuda, before cruising in company to New York for a grand Parade of Sail. It was not easy to borrow a ship for such a venture, but eventually he contacted Lord Boyd at Ince Castle, near Plymouth, who agreed to lend his beautiful bermudan yawl *Tawau* to be raced under the command of James Myatt. The Watch Officers included James Bardon, who was racing aboard *British Soldier* in 1980, David Cobb, who runs much of the Duke of Edinburgh Award Scheme, and John Hamilton, later to become Race Director. The trainees

Short break by the main deck capstan while lowering *Danmark*'s main royal yard

Making *Danmark* fast alongside at Karlskrona: two cadets stand by the double wheels, in the foreground second officer Steffen Schultz, to his right, Captain Otto L. Bentsen

came from all over Britain and were selected aboard *Discovery* in the Thames, a ship well known to Myatt since his childhood. Having chosen the crews, funds and sponsorship had to be raised and eventually *Tawau* set off across the Bay of Biscay, in the Class B race to Lisbon. There she joined eight square-riggers, and three others of her class to compete across the Atlantic.

The competitors became acquainted through radio contact during the crossing, before the festivities in Bermuda. *Danmark* made a notable exit from Hamilton Harbour on that occasion, when, under the command of her Master, Captain Knud Hansen, she sailed from her berth alongside through the narrow cuts, a remarkable feat of seamanship.

During the cruise from Bermuda to New York some ships exchanged crews, and John Hamilton and a number of British cadets joined *Christian Radich*. These informal interchanges were successful and gave the boys (at that time few girls participated) the opportunity of knowing the other competitors.

Tawau gained much publicity in the United States, and, on her return, James Myatt and David Cobb gave lectures on sail training to raise funds for the STA scheme to build a ship for Britain. Meanwhile, Hugh Goodson, then Chairman of the STA, had formed a special committee with the help of many notable authorities on sailing ships, which examined the project. Maldwin Drummond joined the STA and later became Chairman; in 1980 he was a Vice-Patron of the Association. He has also written the official STA reference book on the present sail-training ships of the world, entitled *Tall Ships*, published in 1976 by Angus and Robertson, and illustrated by Mike Willoughby.

After much discussion and some dispute about square- versus fore-and-aft rig, it was decided that a three-masted topsail schooner should be designed by Camper and Nicholson's in association with Captain John Illingworth, FIN, RN. Once this was finalised in November 1964, the keel was laid by Admiral Sir Charles Madden at Hessle and construction began at the yard of Richard Dunston. Shortly before she was due to be launched, she accidentally triggered off the launching mechanism and broke her masts. *Sir Winston Churchill* was launched in March 1966 by Mrs June Goodson.

An office managed by Captain David Bromley-Martin, RN, was set up in Bosham for running the schooner, handling all the bookings and administration as a separate entity from the Tall Ships Race Organisation. Everything had to be planned for the two-week voyages for adventure training from the routines for the trainees to the composition of the permanent crew, the introduction of volunteer watch officers, and day-to-day running of the ship. Captain Glynn Griffiths, who joined the schooner in 1965, was involved with everything. He had much experience in handling ships as well as teaching and working with young people, and had competed in the first Tall Ships Race with Merchant Navy cadets on *Berenice*.

Sir Winston Churchill soon embarked on her training programme of cruises, which continued until the late autumn. She won first prize for her class in the Tall Ships Race from Falmouth to the Skaw—a silver bosun's call presented by HRH Prince Philip, Patron of the STA, and which still sails aboard her.

John Hamilton, STA Race Director, standing by the main rigging on *Danmark* at Karlskrona, listening to a concert given by cadets and trainees from many of the ships for a live radio show in Sweden

The publicity and success of the schooner prompted Sir James Miller, then Lord Mayor of London, to donate £75,000, which he guaranteed to double through other sources, for the building of a sister ship to be named after his son who had died in a car crash. The offer was accepted and in October 1967 *Malcolm Miller* was launched at the yard of John Lewis & Sons of Aberdeen. Glynn Griffiths took over her command and Captain Mike Willoughby joined *Sir Winston Churchill*.

The schooners average 30,000 nautical miles and take 1,250 trainees and 350 adults to sea each year. By the end of 1980, 17,500 trainee berths will have been filled on these ships whose capacity gained 99 per cent usage in 1980. Both joined the tall ships for Race Two at Frederikshavn.

Since the early sixties James Myatt has also been closely involved with the Ocean Youth Club and the London Sailing Project, for which he skippered *GBII* from Bermuda to Boston in 1976. He has actively helped the Royal Yachting Association, and chaired the Yachtmaster Qualifications Panel. He sailed when he was in the Royal Artillery, including skippering the Army entry in 1974 for a leg of the Whitbread Round-the-World Race.

The first organised crew exchange and cruise-in-company, from Malmö to Kiel in 1972, was extremely successful. In 1976, en route to the USA, an exchange of cadets was organised by James Myatt and John Hamilton incorporating a short cruise from Santa Cruz de Tenerife to Los Christianos. Over

STA topsail schooner *Sir Winston Churchill* at the start of the race from Frederikshavn to Amsterdam, 1980 (*Janka Bielak*)

forty vessels took part, including eight Class A ships. Having seen the cadets safely embarked in Santa Cruz, Myatt and Hamilton drove across the mountainous island to Los Christianos, a small fishing port completely unprepared for the invasion. Soon, however, Myatt was directing the international square-rigged and bermudan traffic into the harbour, while Greville Howard took the lines ashore. Amid the strains of *Rule Britannia* everyone enjoyed the fiesta!

In 1980, James Myatt, with the help of Brigadier Codner, a retired Royal Artillery officer, organised an exchange between 300 cadets en route from Karlskrona to Frederikshavn. An interdenominational service was held on Sunday morning at the Admiralty Church, a distinctive red building near the naval base, attended by a congregation of ship's companies, race officials and local inhabitants.

PRIZE-GIVING

On the afternoon of 23 July the prize-giving took place in Stortorget Square, where hundreds of people gathered to see Prince Berthil, uncle of King Carl Gustav of Sweden, make the presentation. Captains, crews and cadets, headed by banners identifying each ship, marched up the crowd-lined streets to the square. There were uniformed sailors from the square-riggers and naval ships, while others dressed in matching and often suitably labelled T-shirts or embroidered

Some of the captains at the prize-giving for Race One at Stortorget, Karlskrona: *(left to right)* Captain Nils Arntsen, *Sørlandet*, Captain Alexey B. Perevozchikov, *Kruzenshtern*, Captain B. Barner Jespersen, *Georg Stage*, Captain Tadeusz Olechnowicz, *Dar Pomorza*, accompanied by two cadets (one behind, and one holding the prize), Captain Bonniou, *Belle Poule*, a French officer, and Captain Cousquer of *Etoile (D. J. Benstead)*

HRH Prince Berthil of Sweden, presenting Captain Kjell Wollter *(right)* and two trainees from *Gratitude of Gothenburg*, with the Florence Cup at Stortorget, Karlskrona *(D. J. Benstead)*

jerseys, or even, as one crew arrived, disguised as pirates! It was impressive to see how many nationalities were represented among the ships and their crews: Ecuadorians, Poles, British, French, Germans, Americans, Canadians, Swiss, Chileans, Russians, Danes, Dutch, Norwegians, and Swedes.

On the steps of the Town Hall the captains were accompanied by one or two cadets to receive their awards from Prince Berthil, who is a keen yachtsman among other members of the Swedish Royal Family.

First to cross the line had been the Chilean yacht *Blanca Estela*, whose prize was collected by Captain John Martin. Second was *Queen,* followed by *Walross III* and *Sabre*.

On corrected time, Captain Tadeusz Olechnowicz of *Dar Pomorza* received first prize for Class A—a glass vase engraved with a ship. Captain Nelson Armas collected the second prize for *Guayas*, and third prize went to Captain Krzysztof Baranowski for *Pogoria*.

The Swedish Cruising Association was well represented in Class B I. Captain Kjell Wollter collected first prize for *Gratitude of Gothenburg*, and second prize went to Captain Gösta af Klint for *Gratia of Gothenburg. Carola* from West

The bows of *Gorch Fock* with its distinctive eagle figurehead

Germany, owned and skippered by Captain Hans-Edwin Reith, was third, followed by *Equinoxe*.

HMS *Falken* in Class B II produced a popular win for the Royal Swedish Navy, especially as she is based at Karlskrona. Her prize was collected by her Captain, Ragnar Westblad. *Etoile* had beaten *Belle Poule* by less than thirty seconds, and *Kranich* had come fourth.

In Class B III the Russian yacht *Ritza* came in first, then *Hajduk* from Poland, *Sparta* from the USSR, and *Queen* from West Germany. At the end of the ceremony Greville Howard raised a rousing three cheers for Prince Berthil, Sweden and the hospitality of Karlskrona.

7

CRUISE IN COMPANY FROM KARLSKRONA TO FREDERIKSHAVN ABOARD *KRUZENSHTERN*

To see four different nations on the wheel of a square rigger in a blow is to understand just what our cruise-in-company can mean when we mix young people from different nations in each other's ships.

LIEUTENANT-COMMANDER, THE HONOURABLE GREVILLE HOWARD, VRD, RNR, STA CHAIRMAN, SAILING (OVERSEAS), *International Silver Jubilee Sail Training Race Programme* (1977)

The great square-rigger *Kruzenshtern*, the largest sailing vessel in commission in the world, dominated the quay. Her masts towered 52 metres (170 feet) above the decks while her yards and rigging were illuminated by electric bulbs. Her cadets had spent many hours preparing this effective spectacle of lights.

On board, as part of the organised exchange of crews, were about eighteen boys and two girls representing ships from the races, including *Symfoni*, *Urania*, *Wojewoda Pomorski*, *Trygław*, *Dar Pomorza*, *Walross III*, *Dusmarie*, *Dasher*, *Cereola* and *Royalist*. Among the other vessels which had also exchanged crews *Sparta* had gained a complement as varied as space would allow—nearly eight nations on about 13.7 metres (40 feet) of boat! *Pogoria* had exchanged all her trainees for nearly forty youngsters, including the first girls to join her. On board *Kruzenshtern* I listened to electric guitar music played by a pop group. A Cuban boy sang a song, followed by an encore. Later, the audience was practically dancing as traditional tunes like *Kalinka* echoed across the decks.

'WITH SHIPS THE SEA WAS SPRINKLED FAR AND NIGH'

Early in the morning we left the quay and headed for the anchorage where we would await the formation of the parade. King Carl Gustav of Sweden was present incognito (owing to a point of protocol—he was due to officiate at Karlskrona's tercentennial celebrations) to view the fleet of sailing ships from a small vessel, while Prince Berthil took the official salute from HMS *Visborg*. Thousands of spectators watched from the shore while the water was bustling with craft of every description.

As the parade began, *Kruzenshtern* raised anchor to take her place among the smaller ships of her group. On board, whistles sounded to order the boys aloft and loud-speakers directed the setting of sails. *Pogoria* was nearby us, then *Hoshi*, *Belle Poule* and *Etoile*. Some way astern, leading the next section, came *Georg Stage* who was heading home to Denmark to continue her training programme.

The jarvis brace winches came into action to trim the yards as we came

The Parade of Sail, Karlskrona, after the harbour festivities: *(centre) Georg Stage*, under full sail; *(left)* the Polish barquentine *Pogoria*, surrounded by many spectator craft

(Left) Russian cadets aboard the four-masted barque, *Kruzenshtern*, during the Parade of Sail at Karlskrona; *(right)* on the same ship, Russian cadets and two English girls stand by, awaiting orders

Carl Phelan on the bowsprit of *Kruzenshtern*, sailing at $13\frac{1}{2}$ knots through the straits between Copenhagen in Denmark and Malmö in Sweden

through the narrow entrance between the barrier of islands. Having saluted Prince Berthil, we left the parade at about 1100, with good visibility and all sails well set in the breeze.

On board *Kruzenshtern* the visiting cadets were to spend two days learning the normal ship's duties and the regular instruction which is part of the Russian cadets' two-month course to qualify for the Baltic Division of the USSR Fisheries Service. The cadets were divided into three groups—one for watch-keeping, one for deck work and the other for lessons—which rotated weekly.

Kruzenshtern normally carries about ten women among her crew, including a doctor, nurse, teacher, cooks, stewardesses and cleaners, but this was the first time that girls had handled the ropes, climbed aloft, taken the wheel and gained some knowledge of the working life of this schoolship.

Each visiting cadet had a Russian boy as a guide and was assigned to a watch to assist with deck duties and sail-setting stations. All the cadets were eager to learn more about each other's ships, although conversation was hindered by language problems. The Russians, however, had English phrase books with relevant nautical terminology.

The four daily meal-times were staggered in order to accommodate the total complement of 270 and to maintain watches on deck. Breakfast began at about

0730, lunch consisting of soup and a hot meat dish followed at midday and at about 1600 there was a savory tea with salad before supper at 2000. Typical accompaniments were the dark Russian bread which was baked on board, and black tea already sweetened for the cadets. In one day alone I reckoned that about 1,000 tomatoes and 270 pots of yoghurt were eaten. A Cuban boy had a birthday one day and shared his cake with the visiting cadets. Each evening films were shown on the mess deck, some about the USSR, but in the officers' mess, aft, the television received Swedish transmissions, including the BBC television series *The Magic of Dance*. The radio could be heard most of the day. The poop was a popular place to relax as permission was given for anyone to smoke there. Dominoes was a favourite pastime and sailors in track suits performed various exercises in the evening, including running laps around the ship.

The visitors also learnt about such tasks as holystoning the decks, which were first scrubbed with sand and bundles of twigs and then swept clean with water. It was always a whirl of activity among the multi-lingual crew who spoke with Latvian, Estonian, Russian, Cuban and other accents from regions as far north as Murmansk beyond the Arctic Circle to Riga, and there was the opportunity to learn a few foreign phrases.

EMERGENCY ABOARD TS *ROYALIST*
The wind allowed us to sail along the Swedish coast and make a good passage which was only interrupted by an urgent call from TS *Royalist*. A girl trainee on board was suffering from suspected appendicitis and the ship was about to return to harbour. Before the crew had prepared to make their detour, however, Captain Perevozchikov offered the facilities on *Kruzenshtern* and the expertise of the ship's doctor to operate if necessary. This offer was accepted and, within an hour, the barque sent over a lifeboat to the brig, which returned with the patient who was hoisted aboard on a stretcher. After examining her, the doctor decided not to operate immediately but she remained on board under observation. By the end of the voyage the inflammation had subsided and I think the girl quite enjoyed the unexpected experience of life on *Kruzenshtern*. Morin Scott, Master of *Royalist*, noted in his radio message of thanks to Captain Perevozchikov: 'It was a fine example of co-operation in the spirit of the brotherhood of the sea.'

ALOFT
Kruzenshtern was now sailing at $13\frac{1}{2}$ knots in the sound between Sweden and Denmark, with Copenhagen to port. Passing *Creole*, we approached Helsingør, famous for Hamlet's castle. Standing at the steering wheel, four cadets worked together, learning to handle the spokes as a team. They took directions from one of the boys who was watching the compass. Four hours on duty was standard but the visitors took a shorter spell. Those on watch at the bows stood by the bell ready to sound warning of any ships sighted to port, starboard or ahead. The time was also marked by the striking of the bell at half-hourly intervals.

Carl Phelan and I made our way up the rigging, accompanied by one of the Russian cadets and a boy from *Royalist*. We reached the futtock shrouds to gain

The British Sea Cadet Corps brig TS *Royalist (The Sea Cadet Corps)*

The *Kruzenshtern* pop group at the Bord Party, Bremerhaven (*Stadtbildstelle Seestadt Bremerhaven*)

the first platform, and then climbed further. From such a height one could appreciate the size of the ship and it was exhilarating to be sailing with the billowing sails all around us. The solidity of the gear was emphasised close to— but we still had to remember to clip our safety lines securely to a strong point, even though fascination diverted the mind from the distance below.

KRUZENSHTERN

Kruzenshtern, originally *Padua*, was built in 1926 at the yard of J. C. Tecklenborg at Geestemünde, Bremerhaven, for the famous Laeisz Flying-P-Line of Hamburg. She made many fast passages carrying nitrates from Chile or wool from Australia, and was the last cargo sailing ship of her capacity to be launched. She is, in fact, the only one at sea today, although her layout has been altered to accommodate numerous cadets instead of a few sailors and apprentices. Her four-masted barque rig has changed little, but the three-island superstructure on her black hull was lost in a major refit made by the Ministry of Fisheries in 1968–73, when she lay at the Kronstadt Shipyard.

In 1946 she was taken over for use by the Russian Navy but was not converted completely, hammocks and bunks simply being lodged below. She worked as an oceanographic survey ship in the mid-Atlantic 1961–5, and at some stage was painted white. The Fisheries Service bought her in 1966 for training, and in 1967 she cruised to Sevastopol. She then underwent a five-year reconditioning, and her hull was painted black with a line of false gun-ports in white.

Kruzenshtern under full sail at the start of the Tall Ships Race from Plymouth to Tenerife, 1976 (*Mike Smith*)

Sedov, another Russian sailing ship, but even larger than *Kruzenshtern*, is now undergoing a similar refit for the same owners. She was previously called *Magdalene Vinnen II* when she sailed under German ownership before World War II. The Captain, Chief Officer and Chief Instructor told me the history of these ships since their Russian ownership.

HMS *FALKEN* AND *DONALD SEARLE*

We were now approaching north Denmark and our destination. Soon the pilot would come aboard to guide us through the narrow entrance into Frederikshavn Harbour. Although many of our fellow competitors were already moored there, others were still arriving. Some of the swifter vessels had enjoyed a leisurely passage and stopped en route at Copenhagen or at a beach for relaxation.

The navigators of HMS *Falken* and *Donald Searle* exchanged places to see if their ships, which had remained in close contact throughout the race, would do so with their course plotters reversed. This exchange and that of their cadets with various other vessels, proved highly successful.

Lieutenant Ragnar Westblad, Captain of HMS *Falken*, remembering during Race One that it was the first anniversary of *Donald Searle*, added a celebratory note when, at midnight, his crew sang 'Happy Birthday' over the radio! Spontaneously, *Donald Searle* sent the following biblical reply:

'And Ruth said: "Intreat me not to leave thee, or to return from following thee: for whither thou goest, I will go; and where thou lodgest, I will lodge: thy people shall be my people, and thy God my God." '

When the crews arrived in Denmark they returned to their own ships. Much had been learnt by the exchange of crews and, as one of the cadets said afterwards: 'Learning to sail, and sail training are different. The former is simply how and why to pull this rope or that halliard—in other words, knowledge in order to do the appropriate thing at the right time. But the latter involves far more: it teaches self-discipline, team-work, and above all the ability to live with others.'

FREDERIKSHAVN

The attractive town of Frederikshavn welcomed the training ships informally with concerts from naval and town bands, the convenience of nearby shops, cafés set up on the quaysides, music in a marquee each evening, a fair and other entertainments.

A brochure about Frederikshavn stated: 'I am the puppy of the Danish towns—long, lanky and lively, and very go ahead.' This North Jutland town, with a population of 25,000, received a municipal charter in 1818 and was named after King Frederik VI. The harbour is important as a route centre, serving ferries to Norway and Sweden, as a major base for the Royal Danish Navy, for shipyards, and as a busy fishing port where there are some excellent restaurants.

The crews spent two enjoyable days in Frederikshavn. The captains and navigators attended an official briefing for Race Two and soon it was time for everyone to prepare for the start of the next race.

8

TO AMSTERDAM ABOARD
DAR POMORZA

Beneath the gloss and the glamour of the Tall Ships under sail, however, is a more practical principle. Those who organised the first Tall Ships Race were not seeking to present a spectacle. They wanted to offer young people an opportunity to face together in friendship and competition the challenge presented by racing at sea under sail. The strict rule was that at least half the crew should be aged between 16 and 26 and undergoing sea training either for a career or character building.

JAMES ANDERSON, *STA Race Programme* (1976)

On 1 August the ships left Frederikshavn and set off for Amsterdam. The Class B vessels departed at a steady pace, while tugs manoeuvred the great tonnage of square-riggers from their basin. Owing to our position in the docks, *Dar Pomorza* was among the last to leave, after *Sørlandet*. We passed through the narrow harbour entrance on the engines and made our way to the starting area. Many other craft were waiting as there were still a few hours to go before they could all cross the line.

We saw the Royal Yacht *Dannebrog*, white and resplendent, with the traditionally elegant lines of a classic motor yacht, decorated with intricate gold 'gingerbread'. Queen Margrethe of Denmark, who was on board with Prince Henrik, was to start the race—royal interest that reflected the Danes' involvement in the event. The view from the Royal Yacht, where the official representatives and organisers joined the Queen must have been rewarding for her.

A conspicuous spectator was the *Danmark*, unable to participate as she was already changing crew for her next training course the following week. With upper yards sent down and many sails unbent, she was there to let guests and members of the Danish Royal Family watch the splendour of the occasion. In the best tradition a fine luncheon was laid on for them before the ships set course across the line.

In Class A were *Creole*, under Danish ownership, with her new mizzen mast distinctly visible, *Dar Pomorza*, one of the oldest, *Gorch Fock, Guayas, Kruzenshtern, Pogoria* and *Sørlandet*. These ships assembled in open water, scattered, until it was time to start at 1500; at quarter-hour intervals afterwards each of the Class B divisions would follow.

From our decks we could see sails of every shape, size and description in all directions. Many of the competitors were familiar after the Baltic events, while others had just arrived. Among the latter were the British Sail Training Association topsail schooners *Sir Winston Churchill*, sailed by a crew of boys under the

Dar Pomorza: reflections on a calm sea *(Henryk Kabat, Gdynia)*

The start of Race Two off Skagen: Queen Margrethe of Denmark *(centre, with dark glasses)* aboard the Royal Danish yacht, *Dannebrog*, standing next to Lieutenant-Commander The Hon Greville Howard *(in shirt sleeves, centre)*. The Queen started the Race *(Janka Bielak)*

command of Captain John Lawson, and *Malcolm Miller*, with girl trainees, commanded by Captain Mark Kemmis-Betty.

Carillion of Wight, the 24 Thames tons, blue bermudan sloop from the spinnaker class, passed by us. She is owned by the Christian Sailing Centre at Dodnor Creek on the Isle of Wight, from where she sails throughout the summer. Her Skipper on this occasion was Charles Gladdis.

THE OCEAN YOUTH CLUB

Master Builder was there representing the Ocean Youth Club whose aims are defined in the following extracts from the articles of the Association:

> *To provide facilities for yachting and boat-sailing at sea and for seamanship and navigation generally as a recreation or leisure time occupation to improve the conditions of life of youth from all parts of the United Kingdom of Great Britain and Northern Ireland.*

These initial concepts later developed:

> *To give young people between the ages of 15 and 21 the opportunity to go to sea offshore, under sail, to foster the spirit of adventure latent in young people, to encourage a wider outlook and greater understanding of other people, and, to use a sailing ship as the classroom and the sea as the teacher to encourage young people to develop a sense of co-operative responsibility for themselves and the community in which they find themselves.*

(Left) The start of Race Two off Frederikshavn with the French gaff topsail schooner *Belle Poule* in the centre and British three-masted topsail schooner *Malcolm Miller* on the right, amidst other competitors; *(right)* STA three-masted topsail schooner *Sir Winston Churchill* in the centre, with *Svanen* of Sweden on the right *(Janka Bielak)*

The wooden gaff yawl, *Duet*, and *(behind)* *Samuel Whitbread*, one of the large white bermudan ketches used by the Ocean Youth Club to take young people to sea *(David James, Ocean Youth Club)*

The club, which was founded in 1960 with two yachts, *Duet* and *Theodora*, owned respectively by The Reverend A. Christopher Courtauld and Christopher St John Ellis, now runs a fleet of seven 22-metre (71-foot) foam-sandwich bermudan ketches, a Nicholson 55, and *Duet*, which is still on loan to the club.

Based at ports around Great Britain and Northern Ireland, these vessels provide sailing for young people each year and in 1980 the club had some 3,000 members, many of whom sail the yachts and help with the winter maintenance work. Cruises generally last for one week, throughout the season, from March to November. One or two of the club yachts make long voyages during the summer, and their cruising grounds have reached as far as the United States, Iceland and Norway. It has also become a regular feature to have a rally: in 1978 the fleet united in Oslo after the race from Great Yarmouth, and in 1981 at Gosport special celebrations will mark the OYC's twenty-first birthday by gathering together their whole fleet—*Duet*, *Falmouth Packet*, *Francis Drake*, *Grania*, *Master Builder*, *Samuel Whitbread*, *Scott Bader Commonwealth*, *Sir Thomas Sopwith* and *Taikoo*.

In twenty years, over 34,000 trainee berths have been occupied in the club fleet. Major decisions are taken by a Board of Governors, while the overall administration is run from Gosport by David James, with a small office staff and permanent skippers.

David James joined as Director in 1977, and at the end of his first year his 'First Impressions' were published in the club journal:

> . . . *the point common to every gathering of anyone connected with the* OYC *is the friendliness and warmth of everyone I have met.*
>
> *The huge potential of the club is another feature. There is nothing quite like the* OYC *anywhere in the world, as far as I can gather. Here we have these lovely big boats, full of young people, who, until they met five minutes before they stepped on board, had never set eyes on each other, who know perhaps little or nothing about ships and the sea, and who will return in seven days' time confident and cheerful, having lived in close quarters with their fellow men, shared common dangers and excitements, shared moments of beauty and pure magic, and who are all, in one way or another, enriched by their experiences. All this will have happened with little or no artificial discipline, with the minimum of formality and the maximum of good humour—which is the great feature of the club.*
>
> *Up-to-date thinking includes the planning of passages to suit modern youth—to extend the challenge of the sea—to use the sea to bring out the best of the very best in Man. There's not a lot of value to be gained in a marina, a disco or a pub—there's immeasurable gain to be found at sea, or anchored in a bay where the crew must provide their own entertainment, and do so, very well.*

OTHER COMPETITORS

Another entrant in the race was *Stormvogel*, a 24-metre (80 foot) LOA bermudan ketch, registered in Austria, based in Italy, and owned by her Polish Skipper, Jacek E. Palkiewicz. A yachting journalist and author, he is an expert on training ships, as well as being a deep-sea captain and single-handed sailor. This yacht was built in South Africa in 1961 for the Dutchman Cornelius 'Kees' Bruynzeel, to designs drawn up by Illingworth, Laurent Giles, Primrose and Van de Stadt. In her prime she gained line honours in many major ocean events, including the Buenos Aires to Rio, Transpacific, Sydney to Hobart, Newport–Bermuda and the notorious Fastnet Races, and she has rounded the Horn more than once. She now concentrates on chartering.

The Captain of HMNLS *Urania* for Race One, Commander Bernard Heppener, left at Frederikshavn to brief the liaison officers he was to be in charge of in Amsterdam. Lieutenant G. Veenman took over, as did Captain Jansen on *Eendracht*. These Dutch entries were joined by *Gre 14, Kanaloa, Mjojo, Ran, Sepha Vollaars, Symfoni, The Great Escape, Tielsa* and *Tineke*.

After Great Britain and the Netherlands, the largest contingent in the second race came from Poland, with *Zew Morza* in Class B II, and *Doris II* in Class B III, together with the following yachts which had already competed in Race One: *Hajduk, Hetman, Roztocze, Trygław, Wodnik II* and *Wojewoda Pomorski*, with, of course, *Dar Pomorza* and *Pogoria* in Class A.

In Race Two, there were also four Colin Archer designed vessels from Norway, including the original *redningsskøyte* (rescue vessel, sail number RS I) which was named after him. Built at Larvik in 1893, *Colin Archer* was the first ship to sail for the Norwegian Lifeboat Association, serving for forty years along the Arctic coast of Norway, without an engine. She gained a fine reputation while on duty, saving 240 lives and assisting 4,500 crew members from a total of 1,500 vessels in distress. Her strong construction, including a double hull, and other seaworthy qualities particularly suited to the waters in which she sailed, led to a fleet of rescue vessels designed by her namesake. Two more of these gaff ketches, RS 5, *Liv*, and RS 10, *Christiania*, were also racing. It is a grand sight to see these rescue craft assembled for a rally, relaxing, one imagines, after a worthy career on duty. They are readily identified by the red circle around their sail numbers and the cross on the bows, which are not unlike the sterns—typical 'double-enders'.

Colin Archer has been completely restored and is beautifully maintained by her Skipper, Knut von Trepka, who takes great care of her for the Colin Archer Sailing Club to which she is entrusted by her owners, the Norwegian Maritime Museum. This club was founded in 1972 for the specific purpose of creating additional interest in this genre of traditional wooden sailing craft, helping to encourage the preservation of those that remain, promoting activities for those which are in commission, and arranging winter meetings at the Norwegian Maritime Museum in Oslo. Although the nucleus of membership is in the area of Oslofjord, there are many enthusiasts further afield and outside Norway.

Another member of the club in Race Two was the gaff cutter *Ledina*. She was built in 1975 to the original drawings of Colin Archer, which had not been used before.

FAMILIAR COMPETITORS

Some of the entrants familiar from Race One included *Carola, Christian Venturer, Dark Horse, Jens Krogh* and *Jolie Brise*, the famous black gaff cutter which won the first Fastnet Race in 1925, and repeated her success in 1929 and 1931.

Cadets sheeting in the mainsail on the
Royal Netherlands naval training ketch
Urania (Koninklijke Marine)

It's a long way up the mizzen mast! Cadets on *Dar Pomorza* bending on a topgallant
sail to the yard approximately 30 metres (100 feet) above the deck

Sextants line *Dar Pomorza*'s foredeck: the watch officer *(with cap)* giving instruction to cadets of the Wyższa Szkoła Morska, Gdynia *(Henryk Kabat, Gdynia)*

This Le Havre pilot cutter had been designed and built for speed when she was launched by Paumelle at her home port in 1913. After her working life and famous racing career, she spent many years in Portugal, owned by Eng Luis de Guimaraes Lobato, his country's representative for the Sail Training Association. He sold her in 1977 to Exeter Maritime Museum in the hope that she would be appropriately maintained and would continue sailing. These aims have been achieved by Dauntsey's School Sailing Club which works through the winter at Exeter Maritime Museum to restore her to first-class condition. The school cruises throughout the summer, mainly in the English Channel; in 1978 and 1980 it entered the Tall Ships Races.

Outlaw, the large black staysail schooner, is owned by the Jugendschiff Corsar eV in West Germany. She takes young delinquents and first offenders to sea from a special village where they are sent for rehabilitation. Since 1978 she has made a long cruise each summer with a carefully selected crew. Under the charge of Captain Peter Schwarz, the aim of helping the youngsters to learn about themselves and others and to acquire a new outlook on life is achieving some success.

There was also *Cereola, El Pirata, Halcyon, Hoshi* and *Joana I* from Canada, an 18-metre (60-foot) LOA black and white yawl which was built in Quebec 1975–7 by her Skipper and co-owner, Antonio Freire.

Nearby us was TS *Royalist* under Commander David Gay, her false gun-ports seeming to elongate her black hull. *Peter von Danzig, Walross III, Belle Poule, Etoile* and *Falken* also graced the start.

DAR POMORZA
After lunch of soup and a hot meat dish, we on board *Dar Pomorza* were on the alert with sails prepared by the boys who went aloft to release the gaskets which lash the sails to the yards. Conditions were fair for the ascent up the rigging, light winds not causing the ship to girate or roll. Soon ropes flaked out neatly on deck—this is extremely important as each one must pay out without hitches—and all bunt- and clew-lines were ready to be released. Staysails were unlashed between the masts and on the bowsprit, where these great expanses of cloth had been neatly stowed. The sheets to restrain the sails and harness the wind were laid out in correct order and cleared for action on the appropriate tack.

The hands aloft by the mast at the upper staysails stood on the cranlines, remembering to keep 'one hand for yourself, and one for the ship', an essential phrase when climbing the rigging. 'Always hold the shrouds, never the ratlines', is another firm rule.

Looking up at the yards one could see the loops of folded cloth, sails not yet set, as all around the decks bosuns checked the layout. Orders were awaited anxiously, especially as we were aboard the winning ship from the Karlskrona race.

On the poop some of the ship's complement not involved in the sail drills stood watching the scene—stewards, pursers, journalists and an official guest who was an avid photographer. All cameras were poised to record the view. *Gorch Fock* was nearby. Engines idled gently, while we waited to set sail.

The steel full-rigged ship *Dar Pomorza* is 1,561 registered tons and 1,784 Thames tons. She was designed and built in 1909 as the *Prinzess Eitel Friedrich* by the shipyard of Blohm and Voss in Hamburg, for the *Deutscher Schulschiff Verein* (German Schoolship Association). At the end of World War I, after a short career in training, she was handed over to France and laid up at St Nazaire until 1921. She was then taken over for use by the *Société Anonyme de Navigation—Les Navires Ecoles Français*—but there is no record of her having sailed. In 1926 her name was changed to *Colbert* before she was sold to the Baron de Forrest who apparently planned to convert her as a private yacht. As this scheme did not get beyond the drawing board, however, she was sold to Poland in 1929 as a replacement for the Merchant Navy training barque *Lwow*.

During December that year, having been renamed *Pomorze*, she left France under tow, without masts or engines, but with a small complement of Polish officers on board, including the First Mate and his honeymoon bride! Gales in the Bay of Biscay nearly proved disastrous but she managed to arrive safely at the Nakskov Shipyard in Denmark in January 1930. There she was completely refitted and overhauled with new gear including masts, rigging and a rudder; also, an engine was installed for the first time—and it was still running in 1980.

In July 1930 she entered her new home port of Gdynia, where her name was changed officially to *Dar Pomorza*, which means 'Gift of Pomerania', as it was the people of this northern region of Poland who donated the funds for her purchase. That summer she went on training cruises in the Baltic, which continued annually, occasionally interspersed with extended voyages.

She visited New York and Brazil in 1931 and the South Atlantic in 1933. She set sail on a round-the-world voyage in 1934 when she called at many ports including Panama, Yokohama, Osaka, Shanghai, Hong Kong, Singapore, Broome and Durban. She rounded Cape Horn en route to the South Pacific in 1937. At the outbreak of World War II she was safely sheltered in a Swedish port and remained there for the duration. She returned to resume her role at the Polish Merchant Navy College in October 1945.

Since then, she has sailed on many cruises throughout the Baltic, in other European waters and the Atlantic. Notable events in her recent career include a visit to Expo 67 in Montreal, and, in 1972, a voyage to the Caribbean and her first entry in the Tall Ships Races which she won over the course from Cowes to Skagen, before attending the Parade of Sail at Kiel. In 1974 she was at Gdynia to greet the training ships that visited her city, as well as racing with them. In 1976 she set sail across the Atlantic in the series of races organised by the STA, revisiting east-coast ports of the United States in 1979 for the anniversary celebrations of two Polish generals who had fought in the American War of Independence. She also participated in the Tall Ships Race from Gothenburg to Oslo via Fair Isle in 1978.

The Wyższa Szkoła Morska (Merchant Navy Academy) at Gdynia has expanded considerably since 1929, when the cadets seldom exceeded 180; now there are 1,800 full-time and 700 extra-mural students. The college was granted the status of a university in 1968. Boys who attend courses at the academy join this

(Left) Dar Pomorza in a gale force wind, Bay of Biscay, 1979: wet, windy and destination windward; *(right)* the author at the bows of *Dar Pomorza* heading south with the help of the Portuguese trades, en route from Plymouth to Tenerife, 1979 *(taken by a cadet on* Dar Pomorza*)*

ship for a short initiation cruise in the autumn before the first term, and return for a three-month voyage the following summer. They must pass their first examinations and the course on board in order to continue with their studies and acquire further experience at sea before they can qualify as an officer.

The routine for the boys on *Dar Pomorza* was split into a three-watch system, running standard four-hour duties with two evening 'dogs'. During the day, lessons were given on seamanship, navigation and English, and there were many opportunities for practical instruction.

Dar Pomorza has had only seven masters since 1930. The longest serving was Extra-Master Kazimierz Jurkiewicz who was in charge 1953–77, and he is respected throughout the sail-training world for his superb seamanship.

In 1980 her Master was Captain Tadeusz Olechnowicz who sailed on her for some years with Jurkiewicz before taking over command. He is thoughtful, competent and a good linguist who fully appreciates the value of teaching and training young people at sea.

During her Polish career, which celebrated its fiftieth anniversary in 1980, this ship has trained over 13,000 cadets, visited hundreds of ports in many countries around the world and sailed over 480,000 sea miles.

Scrubbing every inch of deck on *Dar Pomorza (Henryk Kabat, Gdynia)*

THE START

Only fifteen minutes to starting time. Boys lined the decks awaiting orders. Maciej, Krzysztof, Marek, Tomasz, Leszek, Piotr, Andrzej and Zbigniew—in fact 129 cadets with the skill and muscle power to hoist and trim the sails. Whistles, loud-speakers and walkie-talkies sounded commands along the length of the ship. First the halliards and sheets for the lower topsails on all three masts, had to be made ready to hoist; then upper topsails and fore-and-aft sails. Gradually, as more sail area was displayed, speed increased. We were near the line. Smooth seas reflected a bright sky.

All would be lost if the line was reached within the final minutes. Timing must be precise; probably 160 sails in class A alone were straining to catch the Force 4, WNW breeze. A puff of smoke from the Royal Yacht *Dannebrog* signalled the last five minutes.

Class A congregated at the start, while Class B sailed around the great ships whose mass of canvas swept them into action. On *Dar Pomorza* the noise of hurrying feet resounded as the ropes were led around the deck. Engines were in neutral, and the only power came from the sails which were now billowing above the decks; corrections and adjustments were made to get the advantage over *Gorch Fock* as she came up on our port side with all sail set.

A second puff of smoke fired from the Royal Yacht indicated the start of the race to Holland. Orders in Polish reverberated through the loud-hailers. Once we were well under way the cadets returned to the regular routine of watches, maintenance, lessons and sleep. The Captain, who had his chair placed on deck so that he could oversee everything, checked the trim of the sails. In fact he seldom retired below during the race and usually slept in his day-cabin. The students helped the navigator plot the track on the chart and the Captain made the all-important decisions of when to tack to the best advantage.

After Class A had started, the three divisions of Class B followed in turn. Soon, the sleek advantageous hulls, capped by efficient bermudan rig, disappeared over the horizon to windward. They managed to sail far closer to the wind than the square-riggers and gaffers which fell away from their objective, lengthening the distance they had to travel owing to the nature of their sail plan and design.

At 1700 we were lying at 57° 48′ N, 11° 06′ E, sailing towards the Swedish coast. We tacked off the Maskekar Light 2 hours and 47 minutes later, and headed on a course slightly to the west of south.

Alarms sounded below at 2342: all hands were required on deck to manoeuvre the ship around once again. A smooth operation followed. We had sailed 40 miles since 1700.

In the early hours of the morning the wind was changing to WSW. We were still sailing towards the north into Bohus Bay but the next tack would bring us south again. It was a long beat out of the constricted waters of the Skagerrak or Sleeve, and all around us other ships were also trying to gain the best advantage. As the winds became lighter the conditions became more exasperating, and it was apparent that we had to find favourable currents along the Norwegian coast. *Pogoria* was one ship tempted in that direction.

Dar Pomorza: rigging silhouetted
against the billowing sails

Sail power can be seen! *Dar Pomorza* creaming along at 12 knots with all sail set in the
Portuguese trade winds

Lessons were not always so popular with the boys when the orders to get up to trim sails were more frequent than usual; nevertheless the training routine continued. One day, when Sławomir Maj had time to relax on deck, he explained to me how he had come aboard *Dar Pomorza*, and what it meant to him to sail on this 'treasure of Poland'. He said that it was hard but enjoyable work and the races were a big bonus. He had learnt a great deal about people from other countries, and had made friends with the crews from the other ships, especially since the party at the Ostseehalle.

THE CREW
The cadets lived on the open mess decks where they soon came to know each other. These two open spaces below, one for forty boys, the other for eighty, had lockers for their uniforms and personal gear. At night rows of hammocks filled the whole area. Those with time to sleep in the day had to curl up on deck, either above where the ship's boats provided shelter on the main deck, or below wherever there was a spare corner. During the day the mess decks were cleared, except for the tables, at which the cadets ate and studied.

All eyes on the crew: *(right)* Captain Kasimierz Jurkiewicz, Master of *Dar Pomorza* for many years, with her present Master, Captain Tadeusz Olechnowicz. Photographed in 1976 *(Henryk Kabat, Gdynia)*

On Saturday evening *Dar Pomorza*'s lights shone dimly in the mess deck as officers, petty officers and cadets relaxed and watched a film. In the galley the baker was preparing his regular overnight baking of nearly a hundred loaves. His recipe requires no yeast but is made up of a special form of leavening created by a continual supply of the old dough which is kept in a bin to mature. The loaves are dark, firm, nutritious and have a distinctive flavour. The cook had also baked cakes for Sunday, and, having turned them out of long tins, he cut one while it was still steaming to show me its complex marble patterning. Before long, the boy assistants and I—and a few others— had devoured a whole cake!

Next evening, while a Dutch film crew aboard *Dar Pomorza* were making adjustments to their arc lights which had been lashed in the rigging the ship was suddenly lit up against the darkness of the sky. *Sea Cloud*, which lay to port of us, was obviously impressed for she made a friendly response by switching on her floodlights above her decks for a few moments. Astern to port we could see the lights of *Gorch Fock* and *Royalist*, while *Guayas* lay to starboard.

POSITIONS

Early on Sunday 3 August the weather was calm with only a light breeze to ripple the sea. We listened to the radio schedule to hear where our rivals were placed. All were plotted on our chart for comparison, and then we waited eagerly for corrected positions to be transmitted later in the morning. Both *Gorch Fock* and *Pogoria* were keen competitors and could give us problems.

Cadets setting sail on a windless day in Amsterdam to demonstrate techniques on a square-rigger

Some of the boys were busy lining the decks with sextants to check the changing height of the sun. When conditions are favourable there is always time for practising navigation.

Our position was amid the fleet which was scattered across the sea en route to Amsterdam, second on corrected time in our class, thirtieth overall. *Pogoria* was ahead of us as suspected, and *Gorch Fock* lay third, *Guayas* fourth, *Kruzenshtern* fifth, *Sørlandet* sixth and *Creole* last.

In Class B I *Carola* lay fifth, *Jens Krogh* seventh, *Royalist* sixth, and the four Norwegian double-enders skilfully monopolised the lead in the following order: *Colin Archer, Christiania, Liv* and *Ledina*, which was also first overall.

In Class B II the Canadian gaff yawl *Joana I* was seventh; *Etoile* was ahead of *Belle Poule* which lay fourth; the large Polish gaff schooner *Zew Morza* was second, and *Cereola* was first in her class. *Malcolm Miller* was not placed as she had gone off course to take a sick crew member to a Norwegian port for medical attention.

Some ships were not heard over the radio and some were unable to make contact—particularly the leading yachts which were often too far ahead to do so. Of the Class B III positions which were recorded on 3 August, HMSTY *Sabre* was third, *Ritza* was second, and *Wojewoda Pomorski* first. Some of the ships had not radioed their positions but *Somerset* received an encouraging message: two of the crew received a radio-telephone link call from two girls in Karlskrona arranging a visit to Britain in the near future!

On 3 August, a beautiful day, I climbed up the foremast. One of the Bosuns, Tadeusz Popiel, showed me the way over the futtock shrouds, which present an obstacle similar to an overhang in mountaineering. Feet disappear in an alarming way from sight and all your arm power is needed for the last heave on to the tiny platform. Here the angle is much steeper than on any of the other ships on which I have sailed. Once over that hurdle, the climb up to the second platform with its smaller overhang was easier. I shall never forget the view from the level of the topgallant sails, which were curving gently in the breeze. Far below I could see the boys working on the decks. Ropes and rigging tautened in all directions and their functions fell into place: I could see where these vast metal shrouds, served over with tarred line led and what they supported. All the gear was enormous, the yards massive, but the solidity and firmness were reassuring. I could see no ships on the horizon and it was time to return to duty below.

Tadeusz Popiel is naturally at home in this network after maintaining these miles of rope and wire for thirty years. In the Petty Officers' Mess he introduced me to the Assistant Steward, Kazimierz Dopke, who makes ships in bottles in his spare time. The hobby of the Chief Electrician, Roman Garbacki, is impressing portraits of *Dar Pomorza* on sheets of metal.

SUNDAY EVENING—BECALMED

As the sun sank below the horizon, some of the square-riggers a mile or so away were sailing—but only just, thanks to their royals catching the light kiss of the breeze. *Dar Pomorza*, however, was virtually motionless. The cadets were

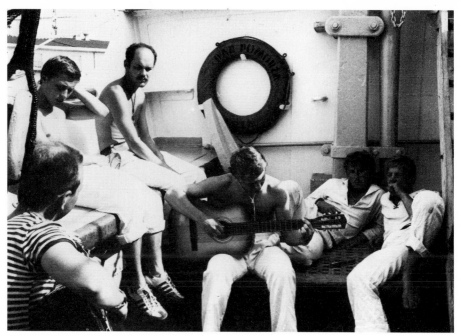

Dar Pomorza cadets relax *(Stadtbildstelle Seestadt Bremerhaven)*

Out on the yards of *Dar Pomorza* and climbing on to the first platform by the over-hanging futtock shrouds where feet disappear at an alarming angle!

occupied on deck with a quiz: two boys from each watch had to answer questions on the sea and ships. The winner and runner-up were awarded packets of cigarettes which were immediately distributed among the audience. Then some of the boys found their guitars and began to play Polish songs which were obviously full of the popular humour and quips; I was sorry that my Polish was not good enough to catch the jokes.

Language was no problem in the next entertainment, however—very high-class dumb crambo. Suddenly the music stopped and another mime show revealed a tennis match. Everyone joined in—the audience, net judge, umpire, ball boys, and, of course, the two star players. It was a match to remember! The next item was the *Dar Pomorza* 'bobsleigh team' tearing down an 'icy slope' in action-packed style. This was followed by a sail-drill mime on an imaginary rope. Suddenly, the real call came for all hands to trim sails. The wind was rising to speed us on our way.

4 AUGUST
Positions were relayed on 4 August. *Dar Pomorza* lay first in Class A, sixteenth overall; *Gorch Fock* was a close second; *Pogoria* third; *Kruzenshtern* fourth; *Sørlandet* fifth; *Guayas* sixth, and *Creole* seventh.

In Class B I *Ledina, Colin Archer* and *Dusmarie* were well placed. *Peter von Danzig* led Class B II, with *Etoile* second, *Zew Morza* third, and *Sir Winston Churchill* fourth. In the reports received, in Class B III, *Dasher* was first, followed by *Sabre* and *Hetman*, but this was not a true picture as some of the leaders were not heard.

The weather was still light and most skippers realised that the majority of ships would not arrive in Amsterdam on 6 August for the planned Parade of Sail from the locks at IJmuiden along the North Sea Canal to the city. The STA Race Committee decided that the race was to continue, however, although some vessels retired at this stage, and others were forced out of the running the next day when conditions completely changed and strong westerly head winds compelled those with poor windward performance to run for shelter in Danish harbours.

I was out on the bowsprit, watching the waves as the wind began to pick up gradually, listening to the swish of the water on the bows as the ship sliced sleekly through the breaking sea.

With a contrary wind we were close-hauled, beating forwards with the great 'Fok' or forecourse brought hard down on to the foredeck with the help of the powerful capstan. The yards were pulled in as far as possible against the shrouds. A square-rigger can sail an average of some 65–70 degrees to the wind.

The wind was now increasing after the long calm. Up aloft the sails were showing signs of that comfortable curve which indicated that the wind was pushing the ship on her way.

It was my turn for duty at the wheel. I insisted that the orders were to be given in Polish so that I could improve my knowledge of the language. Smiling boys wondered how it would work out, but all went well with four of us at the two

Spray breaking over *Dar Pomorza*'s fo'c'sle and the port look-out, while she beats to windward. Note the shadows of the footropes silhouetted against the sunlit sails (*Henryk Kabat, Gdynia*)

Six cadets at the double wheels of *Dar Pomorza*, in a strong breeze, sailing from Plymouth to the Canary Islands in 1979

wheels. One of the cadets on the after wheel stood beside me giving the orders as he could read the giro compass course. The ship was steady and there was now sufficient wind for her to have full steerage way.

We continued to creep towards the line on account of the wind which caused us to side-step: at one moment we were aiming for Scotland, at the next for Heligoland. At 1530 Scheveningen Radio issued a gale warning for Dutch coastal waters—south-westerly, Force 7.

Having heard the forecast, the Captain ordered the alarm to be sounded. At 1655 all hands were summoned, all hatches were to be fastened and the safety lines to be rigged. A network of ropes were rigged along the length of the main deck on either side, and more on the poop, to provide a grip as the movement of the ship increased. The hatches leading to the two mess decks were battened down, the cowls removed and flat boards sealed with canvas and large metal bars around the coamings. The wind increased; we were now making over 10 knots, steering 280 degrees close-hauled.

All sails were set until 1715, when the royals were lowered for a passing squall. There was lashing rain and poor visibility, but it was all soon over, and sails were raised again.

With the strengthening wind the atmosphere on board had become charged with exhilaration. We remembered we were in a race, and although the aim of reaching the line on time was now beyond us, we were at least going to give of our best.

Dar Pomorza was now over 45 miles south-west of the Hanstholm Light, leading *Gorch Fock* by nearly 20 miles, but still far from the finish. *Pogoria* lay 70 miles ahead of us.

While we still sailed unavoidably in a zigzag pattern, our aim was to gain as much westing as possible and then, as the wind veered, to take advantage of it to sail south. The weather pattern had to be carefully studied in the interests of our course, safety and seamanship. We could not risk sailing too near the dangerous shoals on the coast near Heligoland and on the notorious Frisian Islands in case of a sudden change in wind direction.

The wind increased and the conditions on *Dar Pomorza* were wet and uncomfortable. The cadets had difficulty in keeping food on their plates, there was some seasickness, and they looked progressively more tired and dishevilled.

At 2315 watches below were roused by the call for all hands. The tired crew made their way on deck under the dimmest of lights. Orders were given to man staysails, spanker, sheets and braces. There was activity on all sides—the ship was tacking.

5 AUGUST

On the final day of the race the weather improved. A breakfast of Polish sausage, home-baked bread, cold meats, tomatoes, jams and tea was served at 0730. The Chief Steward, Michal Liberski, set the table for the Captain and senior officers in his elegant saloon which was filled with souvenirs from many ports of call.

At 0800 I visited the wireless room for the latest news. Wojciech Rekawek, the Radio Officer, had already collected reports from the Polish yachts and some other competitors in order to relay them to *Somerset* which was not able to receive them direct. (It was the initiative of the larger vessels with powerful transmitters that helped to maintain communication, usually through VHF but also on MF.)

Wojciech Rekawek's services to the fleet, which were in addition to his normal duties, were recognised in Amsterdam when he was presented by Cutty Sark with cuff-links embossed with the Tall Ships logo. His normal day's work was to record weather forecasts in morse and clear and to place radio-telephone link calls for the journalists who were aboard to cover the events. Although Poland has a relatively small coast, the news was listened to eagerly.

We heard from the other vessels only intermittently on the VHF as the fleet was now so spread out. Official placings were not given, but we had a fair idea: *Pogoria* was definitely in the lead, followed by us and then *Gorch Fock*, presumably close behind. We had only sixteen hours to improve our position.

Meanwhile, some vessels had retired including *Creidne, El Pirata,* and *Royalist* sailed by Commander David Gay who was eager to arrive in time to change her crew, knowing how long it would take to motor to Holland. *Somerset* was anxious to find *Le Papillon,* which was without an engine, in case she required assistance.

THE FINISH

At almost midnight—our deadline for finishing the race—we were sailing

(Left) Dar Pomorza's starboard anchor secured against the foaming seas at the bows

(Right) The ship's bell on the fo'c'sle of *Dar Pomorza* which was presented to her after her success in the 1972 Tall Ships Race from the Solent to Skagen.

southwards, but still straining to keep a reasonably direct course in the hope that we were ahead of our nearest rivals. Although the wind had been unfavourable we were lying quite well, having made our way to the west before the wind veered.

Now it was a matter of seconds. Stop watches were out and all hands were ready on deck after the alarm had been sounded. Then we passed the finishing time and recorded our position exactly. The crew gave three rousing cheers for the Captain. The order was given for all sail to be stowed: each was bunted and clewed up from the deck, one after another, and then the boys climbed aloft to roll the heavy, slippery cloth neatly on to the yards and make it fast with gaskets.

The fifty-year-old engine came to life to speed us on our way. We were already late for the festivities which were due to begin with a Parade of Sail that day. We made for IJmuiden, the port of entry to the North Sea Canal and Amsterdam, but it still was over 150 miles away even on a direct course. With the wind against us, the windage on masts and yards, powered by an engine that was only auxiliary, we had to beat our way to windward, tacking at intervals, and only made 3–4 knots.

Now we had time to go over the race in our minds, remembering how tired we had been at times. Nevertheless, we had achieved our goal under the skilled leadership of the captain and his officers.

In the radio-room we waited to hear the placings of the other ships, and to pass on to *Somerset* our own position and those of the competitors nearby. We made contact on Medium Frequency, and reported that at midnight we had finished at 54° 14′ N, 06° 20′ E, approximately 28 miles north of the Borkum Riff Light Vessel. Soon we heard that *Pogoria*, our closest rival in Class A, was only 14 miles

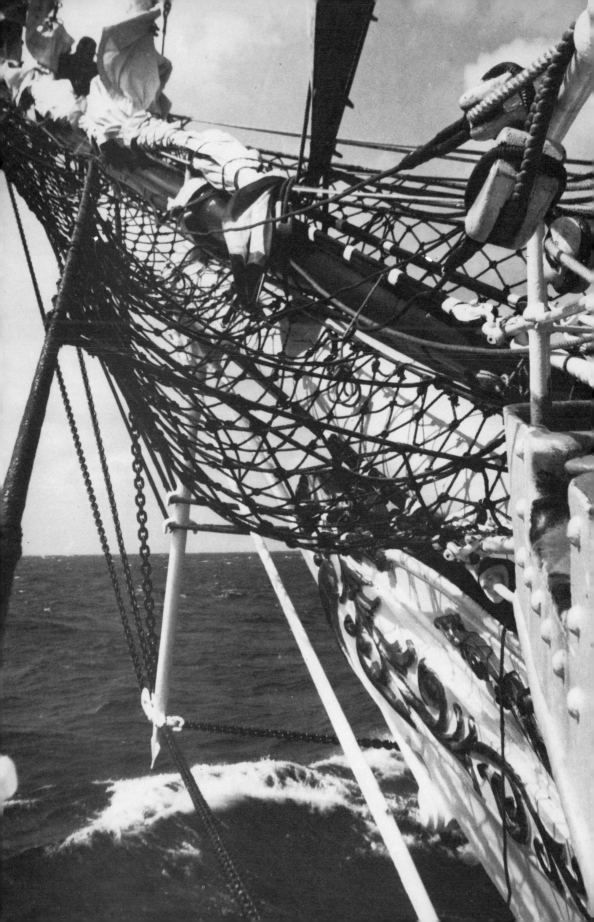

Stowing the topgallant on the mizzen mast of *Dar Pomorza* while sailing close to the wind, yards braced well round on starboard tack. Gaff of spanker visible to left of picture

to the east of us. Baranowski had been beating into the strong westerly wind all day to little avail, while we had been able to set a course southwards and had gained more than 60 miles on her in 16 hours. Our tactics, thanks to our Captain's judgement, had worked. *Gorch Fock* lay about 12 miles astern of us and we estimated the ratings would place her behind us also on corrected time. *Sørlandet* was near *Kruzenshtern* and we knew that *Creole* and *Guayas* had already retired. The latter was towing *Le Papillon* in rough conditions. It was exciting to see the ships' positions being plotted on the chart, but we could be sure of nothing until the results were officially declared in Amsterdam, for each class had a different finishing time, and each ship a different rating.

The most interesting navigational liaison exchanges that I have ever heard then came over on the VHF: '*Sir Winston Churchill, Sir Winston Churchill, Sir Winston Churchill*, this is *Sparta, Sparta, Sparta*, calling . . .' We switched to the appropriate channel and heard that, although *Sparta* had a Decca Navigator on board, she did not have the particular latticed charts for the area. As she wished to obtain a spot-on fix at the finish, she was asking the *Churchill* to help.

Finally, we settled down to a long beat under power and it was over thirty-six hours before we arrived at the locks at IJmuiden.

Details of bowsprit and jib-boom of *Dar Pomorza* showing the gingerbread on the bows, dolphin striker with jib-boom martingales attached, and safety netting. Some sails are stowed as the ship is running before the wind and they would only be blanketed by other sails if set. The massiveness of the gear is indicated by the figure seated on the jib-boom between two sails

The Italian naval full-rigged ship, *Amerigo Vespucci* (*The Italian Navy*)

9

SAIL AMSTERDAM

I once wrote, not altogether in jest, that we are in business to provide memories. The Sail Training Association is convinced that these gatherings make an important contribution to international friendship and understanding among hundreds of young people who take part.
LIEUTENANT-COLONEL, THE LORD BURNHAM, DL, JP, *Tall Ships Race Programme* (1978)

On the morning of Wednesday 6 August the banks of the North Sea Canal were lined with onlookers and there were hundreds of craft waiting to see the first ships arriving. Although we were not there I managed to watch the Parade of Sail from IJmuiden to Amsterdam on television, while at sea we beat our way slowly towards our destination against the unrelenting head winds. More than 200 traditional flat and round-bottomed boats joined this parade, making up for the absence of all but two of the tall ships.

The bermudan racers which had crossed the line in time—*Blanca Estela, British Soldier, Dasher* and *Walross III*—received a great welcome, although they were dwarfed by the four-masted barque *Sea Cloud* and the Italian naval full-rigged ship *Amerigo Vespucci*, which had recently arrived from the Mediterranean. Her distinctive, massive black hull, which is decorated with two white bands, was built in Italy in 1931 for the Italian Navy, and she still serves as a schoolship for training Italian naval officers. She is 4,100 tons displacement, 100 metres (328 feet) LOA, has a beam of 15 metres (51 feet) and carries a total complement of at least 450 men. Her motto is: 'Not he who just starts, but he who perseveres to fulfil his task.'

She has cruised over 400,000 nautical miles and is not the only sailing ship in the Italian Navy. It also owns *Palinuro*, a 1,300 tons displacement barque based in Sardinia to train ratings, and the 21-metre (70-foot) yawls *Corsaro* and *Stella Polare*, which have both entered past races, although they remained in the Mediterranean for the last few years. Captain G. Iannucci, the Commander of *Amerigo Vespucci* in 1980, had also skippered both these latter yachts on long cruises in the Atlantic and Pacific Oceans and in the Baltic. In 1976 *Stella Polare* under Captain Faggioni was in the transatlantic Tall Ships Race and had the distinction in Bermuda, believe it or not, of holing a British warship with her spinnaker pole just before the start of the race to Newport, Rhode Island. Later, Captain Faggioni did express some satisfaction over at last achieving with a spinnaker pole the aim of the Italian Navy during World War II.

When we arrived over a day late on Thursday 7 August, many people were standing on the canal side and we were followed by many boats sounding sirens and fog-horns—we were, in fact, greeted by an overwhelming cacophony. Waving enthusiastically, we passed the spectators, *Somerset* and fellow competitors, and then docked.

Soon a naval launch approached carrying a welcoming party, with Greville Howard, John Hamilton and Janka Bielak. Later we were to meet Admiral, Sir Rae McKaig, KCB, CBE, Chairman, Sailing (UK), Lord and Lady Burnham, Maldwin Drummond, DL, JP, and other officials of the STA, who were in Amsterdam for the festivities.

Sail Amsterdam was organised by a committee, under the chairmanship of Cees H. Goekoop, including John H. J. van Doorn, Secretary, C. Stants, Finance Officer, and Captain C. J. Muilwijk, Harbour Master and technical adviser. Commander Bernard Heppener, with the support of the Royal Netherlands Navy, was in charge of the liaison officers, whose duty was to ensure that the ships were properly looked after. Their role was vital, for the complexity of the docking arrangements alone was considerable. The smaller boats had to be moored three and four deep, even though the quays at Amsterdam are extensive—as all who visited particular ships on foot know. *Gorch Fock* lay ahead of us, and then *Guayas*, who had continued to tow *Le Papillon* until she reached the harbour, where a meal was waiting for her crew aboard *Royalist*. Meanwhile, owing to the bad weather, many ships were yet to come, while others would not arrive at all. *Creidne*, the Irish Sail Training ketch, skippered by Len Breewood, had retired to a port in Denmark, from where the crew had travelled south by train to Amsterdam, arriving in time for the festivities. Her regular skipper, Eric Healy, was sailing aboard *El Pirata* during the race but was due to return to *Creidne* afterwards. However, he had just bought a railway ticket to travel to 'somewhere in Denmark', as he mysteriously put it in order to find her.

Svanen of Stockholm had also sheltered in Denmark, and only arrived in Amsterdam, as did *Ran*, as the majority of ships were leaving. Sadly, the Dutch bermudan ketch *Kanaloa* was lost off the notorious Frisian Islands, but all on board were taken off safely.

Carillion of Wight, an early arrival, was damaged when she hit an unmarked submerged object in the harbour, and had to go to a yard for repairs.

Brilliant timing and drill enhanced the vast red, white and blue spinnaker carried into the IJhaven by the Royal Netherlands Naval ketch *Urania*, and later that evening when *Kruzenshtern* slipped into her berth, 'illuminated overall', a touch of magic was added to the scene.

PRIZE-GIVING

We assembled near the IJhaven on Friday afternoon and prepared for the parade to the Nieuwe Kerke for the prize-giving for Race Two. Having found our place and lined up behind our ship's national flag, we set off at walking pace to the sound of music from a Dutch jazz band. The tram-lines were cleared of traffic and our course took us past Central Station and along the Damrak to the square where, having passed the Royal Palace, crowds watched the colourful procession

The Dutch naval ketch *Urania* carrying her vast, red, white and blue spinnaker as she did into IJhaven at the end of Race Two *(Koninklijke Marine)*

The prize-giving at Amsterdam: Queen Beatrix of the Netherlands presenting Captain Tadeusz Olechnowicz (accompanied by two cadets from *Dar Pomorza*) with the treasured Cutty Sark Trophy in the Nieuwe Kerke in Amsterdam. The Hon Greville Howard and John Hamilton of the Sail Training Association stand respectively behind her and on her left *(National Foto—Persbureau B.V., courtesy of Cutty Sark Scots Whisky)*

Sail drill in Amsterdam aboard
Dar Pomorza

as we entered the contrasting coolness of the recently renovated church. Under the high Gothic windows representatives from the crews of each ship united in an atmosphere of international camaraderie.

The orchestra struck up while we awaited the entrance of Queen Beatrix who was presenting the prizes. A short concert of nautical music followed the Queen's arrival. She was accompanied by the Burgomeister of Amsterdam, Cees Goekoop and Greville Howard, who made the welcoming speeches. John Hamilton announced the award list, while two of the boys from *Somerset* handed over the prizes laid out on the baize-covered table below the chandeliers.

In Class A, fourth prize was awarded to *Sørlandet*, third to *Pogoria*, second to *Gorch Fock,* and first to *Dar Pomorza*.

Guayas received a special prize for travelling the furthest in her class to reach the races—a round trip of at least 12,000 nautical miles.

Christian Venturer was second in Class B I, the remaining places having been taken by the Norwegian double-enders. *Colin Archer* was fourth, with her sister ships *Christiania* placed third and *Liv* first. Unfortunately, *Liv* missed this special occasion as school terms demanded her return to Norway after the finish. *Colin Archer* received a cow-bell, one of the three Bavarian prizes given to the STA in Karlskrona, and the fourth places in Class B II and B III, *Ramrod* and *Blanca Estela* respectively, received Bavarian beer tankards.

Peter von Danzig was first in B II division but was not present to receive her barometer prize because she had broken her mast after the finish and was being repaired in a northern Dutch port before returning to Hamburg. *Etoile* was second and *Falken* third in this class.

The Nicholson 55 *Dasher*, crewed by the Royal Navy, won Class B III, with her sister ship *British Soldier*, sailed by the Royal Artillery, a close second. *Hajduk*, the Polish sloop, was third.

The final prize in the official presentation, the Cutty Sark Trophy, went to *Dar Pomorza*. This silver model of the famous clipper is the greatest honour to be awarded, as all the competing captains vote for the ship which they feel has achieved most in the cause of furthering international friendship and understanding—the essence of the races.

Our Captain, Tadeusz Olechnowicz, now delivered a short speech and he revealed a secret that had been kept since Kiel: Greville Howard was to be presented with a silver salver on which had been inscribed: 'To Father, from the Family' and 'Hear, ye children, the instruction of a father and attend and know understanding' (Proverbs, 4:1) and it was accompanied by all the ships' names signed by their captains. The presentation was made on behalf of 'his sail-training family' in recognition of his enthusiasm and energy, and in admiration of the international understanding he generates.

After the prize-giving, Cutty Sark gave a party on board *Dar Pomorza*.

Traditional Dutch vessels lying outside the Norwegian full-rigged ship *Sørlandet* at the festival of Sail Amsterdam

CUTTY SARK AND SPONSORSHIP

Berry Brothers and Rudd, the proprietors of Cutty Sark Scots Whisky, were represented throughout the races by Mr and Mrs John Rudd, Mr F. C. D. Green, JP, and Mrs Green (whose two daughters joined *Pogoria* in the crew exchange), R. E. Cecil, and Oliver Pemberton, the Publicity Controller, with John Murphy as the official Press Officer.

The famous clipper berthed at Greenwich inspired the naming of Cutty Sark Scots Whisky in 1923, when, at 3 St James's Street, London, the headquarters of Berry Brothers and Rudd Ltd, the partners of this family wine and spirits merchants discussed plans to put a new high quality blend of whisky on the market. James McBey, a well-known Scottish artist, had been invited to design a label for this new blend and it was he who suggested that Cutty Sark would be an appropriate name. At that time the Scottish-built clipper had been much in the news as she had been bought by a Captain Dowman who was preparing to use her for training boys at Falmouth. It was therefore agreed that James McBey should design a yellow label depicting an impression of the ship.

Since its introduction, Cutty Sark Scots Whisky has become a bestseller in the USA and is now one of the world's leading whiskies. In 1971 the firm won the Queen's Award for export achievement. In 1972 Colonel Dick Scholfield, then STA Race Director, approached John Rudd, a keen sailor, for financial support for the organisation of the Tall Ships Races, and so began sponsorship by Cutty Sark. The objectives of the races are epitomised by the Cutty Sark Trophy, which was awarded to *Kruzenshtern* in 1974, to *Zenobe Gramme* from Belgium in 1976, when she towed *Kukri* and *Erika* for over 800 nautical miles across the Atlantic to Bermuda, and to *Gladan* in 1978 in recognition of her ambassadorship and goodwill.

The STA cannot rely on sponsorship alone, and fund-raising in other ways is also necessary. Stalls were selling official souvenirs marked with the STA logo—at a great rate, keeping Tony Bell and his wife, and their many energetic helpers fully occupied.

The logo's design was originally produced in America. It is used with the permission of the American Sail Training Association and is the registered emblem of ASTA and STA. It enables Tall Ships International to raise money for the STA by marketing products bearing the logo or by charging a licence fee to firms that wish to use it on, or in relation to, their products. STA volunteers who run stalls at the race ports mainly sell T-shirts, scarves, lapel badges, car stickers and postcards, and all profits help to finance the Tall Ships Races.

SOCIAL LIFE

At Amsterdam one evening I was invited, along with other guests, aboard the gaff schooner *Belle Poule*. One of the cadets who sang to a guitar was making history as the first girl to join this ship for the passage to Brest. This was typical of the kind of informal happy parties that were held on board the ships in the evening and they generated goodwill all round, overcoming political barriers in a way that could not possibly have been otherwise achieved.

(Left) Schooner *Eendracht* under sail with triangular raffee, square fore-sail, and bermudan mainsail set, taking HRH Princess Margriet for a sail past the fleet while cadets on *Kruzenshtern (right)* still stand to attention on the yards after the salute. Note the crowds of spectator craft and *Sea Cloud*, lying ahead of *Kruzenshtern*

Traditional Dutch vessel sailing past *Guayas (left)* and *Amerigo Vespucci (right)*

Spectators lining the decks of the Danish three-masted staysail schooner *Creole* as HRH
Princess Margriet sails past aboard *Eendracht* at Amsterdam

The cadets and officer painting *Dar
Pomorza* illustrate the proportions of the
ship's fisherman's anchor. Note the pot of
paint on the anchor stock; the boy on a
bosun's chair and wearing a safety harness
is painting the gingerbread (*Stadtbildstelle
Seestadt Bremerhaven*)

Tens of thousands came to see Sail Amsterdam

It's 44 metres (144 feet) up to the top of
the main topgallant mast truck on *Dar
Pomorza*

On Friday 8 August there was a special race in which cadets and trainees from the tall ships joined the traditional Dutch sailing craft on the IJsselmeer. It was organised by the Royal Netherlands Yacht Club in co-operation with the Federation *Oud Nederlandse Zeilschepen*. Over 200 competitors and 500 youngsters in the crews took part—the largest gathering of its kind. That evening, the boats moored alongside the tall ships in the IJhaven and the following night many participated in a mock sea battle, a Dutch festival dating back to the fifteenth century. Lights, flares and sounds were part of the action, while a firework display illuminated the night sky.

On Sunday these craft set sail past the Dutch schooner *Eendracht* anchored in the IJhaven, where Princess Margriet took the salute. Jibs dipped in unison as the vessels passed in line abreast, their long coloured burgees identifying the classes flying from the end of each curved gaff: orange for the Association of Flat and Round-Bottomed Yachts, green for the Botter Behoud, and blue for the Netherlands Sailing Museum Ship Association. Over 200 of these beautifully maintained *boiers, botters, Fries jachts, hoogaars, lemsteraken, schouws, schokkers, tjalks, tjotters,* among others came from all over Holland.

FINALE

Sail Amsterdam was coming to a close; shanties could be heard on the decks of many ships, the Russian pop group played aboard *Kruzenshtern*, and a first-class jazz band performed aboard *Sea Cloud*; a green and white striped awning decorated the stern of *Amerigo Vespucci*; Polish tunes rose from the decks of *Zew Morza* and the mess deck of *Dar Pomorza*, and, on the fo'c'sle of the latter, the *Scheldeloodsenkoor* of pilots from Flushing, accompanied by musicians, sang traditional shanties.

The final evening provided a barbecue which, for those lucky enough to obtain tickets, proved memorable, even though the rain tried to dampen the charcoal fires. Everyone from admiral to burgomeister, cadet to bosun, could be found sheltering under the trees, while kebabs, sausages and chops were roasting. Shanty singing and a jazz band added to the enjoyment. It was a splendid conclusion to Sail Amsterdam, demonstrating that 'The sea can be our bridge'.

Tall Ships registered logo shared by the Sail Training Association and the American Sail Training Association and used to publicise and raise funds for the Tall Ships Races and sail training *(Tall Ships International)*

10

AFTER AMSTERDAM

By the end of the race we had matured into a family of friends which would last a lifetime.

CLARE FRANCIS

Many of the ships left Amsterdam in an official parade on 12 August, and although it was a grey, misty day, spectators still turned out to watch. After the departure from the locks, new destinations and courses separated friends of many nations who were now too occupied setting sails against the squally winds to feel the sadness of leave-taking.

Guayas was heading for Cadiz against a strong westerly wind, en route for Ecuador. *Blanca Estela* was cruising to Lymington in Hampshire before being shipped home, while her crew would fly back to Chile to resume naval duties. *Belle Poule* and *Etoile* were sailing to Brest, their home port in Brittany, while HMS *Falken*, which I joined for the parade, would make a fast voyage to Gothenburg with a fair wind, and later cruise around the archipelago.

Other ships also turned for home, which ranged from the coasts of Britain to Denmark, Holland, Ireland, Italy, Norway, Poland, Sweden, the USSR and West Germany. Some with longer passages to plot—*Christian Venturer, Le Papillon, Lindo* and *Svanen of Stockholm*—remained in Amsterdam to prepare for voyages via the English Channel to warmer climates, starting at Spain and Portugal before setting course across the Atlantic to Bermuda and the West Indies. The Canadian yawl *Joana I* decided to winter in Portugal, while *Stormvogel* returned to her base in Italy to prepare herself for participation in the Whitbread Round-the-World Race in August 1981, which *Walross III* was also planning to enter.

Some enjoyed a final few days of festivity together at Windjammer 80, organised by the city of Bremerhaven in West Germany, in co-operation with the STA. It was a momentous occasion for *Kruzenshtern* to return to the city where she was built. Crews from her cargo-carrying days under sail as the *Padua* travelled from all over Germany to see their ship return. Captain Perevozchikov presented the German Maritime Museum with an original serial number plate from the ship together with details of her Russian career; in return the museum gave a copy of the ship's pre-war history.

Bremerhaven was founded in 1827 by Johan Smidt, Mayor of Bremen; incorporating much older settlements, it has since expanded as a port and city with a population in 1980 of 143,000. Between 1834 and 1927 over 250 large sailing ships were built for trade at seven yards there. Today, the stationary barque *Seute Deern* lies with other exhibits alongside the quay near the German Maritime Museum which houses the Cog of Bremen. The visiting ships were welcomed by Werner Lenz, the Lord Mayor, and Hennig Goes, who was organising the events.

Another cause for celebration was the centenary of the birth of the German naval poet Johann Kinau, who wrote under the pseudonym of Gorch Fock, and after whom the barque is named. An official reception took place and commemorative stamps were issued to mark the occasion.

On Thursday 14 August the vessels participated in a Windjammer parade on the Weser. *Gorch Fock, Dar Pomorza, Kruzenshtern, Pogoria* and *Sørlandet* represented the square-riggers. Other ships included *Albatros, Carola, El Pirata, Olifant* and *Outlaw. Astarte* and *Grønland* were also there, Bremerhaven being their home port.

On Saturday 16 August the latter two vessels contested their annual race. *Astarte* came in first to win a painted sea-chest, while *Grønland* took the consolation prize of a barrel of beer. That evening, during the 'bord' party for all the crews, everyone joined in singing shanties, under the direction of Gunther Bockelmann, and were then entertained by a German Navy choir, a Jamaican limbo band, the pop group from *Kruzenshtern* and a United States Army band. The following day the ships left the port for home.

THE GROWTH OF SAIL TRAINING

'The torch of sail training glows with a bright light, here and there.' So wrote Alan Villiers in the Preface to the *Cruise of the Conrad*, published in 1956, the year of the first Tall Ships Race. By 1980 the value of sail training for character training had come to be recognised as never before. In fifteen years the STA schooners *Sir Winston Churchill* and *Malcolm Miller* have taken 17,500 trainees to sea. In 1980 the Swedish Cruising Association (Svenska Kryssarklubbens Seglarskola) organised sail training for over a thousand young cadets aboard *Gratia, Gratitude* and *Leader*. TS *Royalist* of the Sea Cadet Corps takes an average of 800 cadets on board from March to November. The Ocean Youth Club has filled over 34,000 berths for trainees on the club yachts since its inception in 1960.

New sail-training ships are being built even today. *Asgard II*, a wooden brigantine, has been under construction for two years at the yard of John Tyrrel & Sons at Arklow in the Republic of Ireland. Due to be launched in early 1981, she is 25 metres (82 feet) LOA, and will carry a crew of twenty-five for Coiste an Asgard, the Irish Sail Training Committee.

At Karstensen's Shipyard in Skagen, Denmark, the eventual successor for *Gratitude of Gothenburg* is being built on similar lines—a traditional wooden West Country (British) sailing trawler for the Swedish Cruising Association, and she will be ready for sailing in 1981.

In India, the brigantine *Varuna*, sister ship to TS *Royalist*, has been built for the Indian Sea Cadet Corps, and will be commissioned in 1981.

Ji Fung was launched in October 1980 for the Outward Bound School of

The Parade of Sail heading down the North Sea Canal to IJmuiden at the end of Sail Amsterdam. The white-hulled vessel on the left is *Gorch Fock* while *Amerigo Vespucci* is in the right foreground. The grey day did not keep away countless spectator craft

The twin French naval schooners, *Belle Poule* and *Etoile*, at the locks at IJmuiden leaving the North Sea Canal for Brest

Bremerhaven fire boats celebrate the Windjammer Parade. *(Centre)* the gaff cutter *Grønland* and *(right)* the German naval barque, *Gorch Fock (Luftfoto: Wolfhard Scheer)*

Captain Alexey B. Perevozchikov at the wheel of *Kruzenshtern* (ex-*Padau*) with Frau Christine von Mitzlaff-Laiesz who launched *Padua* in 1926 at the Tecklenborg yard at Bremerhaven, where she revisited the ship in 1980 *(Wolfhard Scheer, Nordsee-Zeitung)*

The prize-giving at the Bremerhaven Bord Party for the annual *Astarte* versus *Grønland* race: in 1980 *Astarte* won the traditional painted sea-chest for first prize, while *Grønland*'s crew were consoled with the barrel of beer. Seated on the sea-chest *(left)* Captain Manfred Hövener, Master of *Grønland*, and *(right)* Klaus Walter Rode, Master of *Astarte*. Behind him, bearded, Harald von Forstner *(Stadtbildstelle Seestadt Bremerhaven)*

Model of *Dar Młodziezy*, the full-rigged ship which will eventually replace *Dar Pomorza* for the Wyższa Szkoła Morska (Merchant Navy Academy) at Gdynia (*Wyższa Szkoła Morska, Gdynia*)

Hong Kong, where this 33.5-metre (100-foot) LOA wooden brigantine was built. *Ji Fung*, which means Spirit of Resolution, was designed by John Brooke, who also similarly designed *Spirit of Adventure*, which sails from Auckland, New Zealand.

There is sail-training activity in numerous countries and many organisations, for instance, the Girl Scouts of the USA are looking for sail-training vessels. Mariners International is seeking to purchase a traditional sailing vessel. Ships are also being restored and recommissioned—for instance, in the USSR it is hoped that *Sedov* will sail again in 1982.

In Poland there are plans to build a new square-rigger, a full-rigged ship of 106.6 metres (350 feet) LOA, of design displacement 2,946 tons, to carry 46 permanent crew and 150 cadets for the Wyższa Szkoła Morska (Merchant Navy Academy) at Gdynia and to continue the traditions of *Dar Pomorza*. Most probably, she will be called *Dar Młodziezy*, which means Gift of Youth.

In Britain plans are under way for building the Jubilee barque, 41 metres (135 feet) LOA, for crews of mixed abilities. There will be six permanent crew and thirty trainees, of whom half will be disabled.

Simon Bolivar was launched in Spain in 1980 for the Venezuelan Navy. She is of similar design to *Gloria* and *Guayas* which were built at the same Spanish yard.

There are also plans in Portugal and other countries to expand their sail-training programmes and to celebrate in 1988 the bicentenary of the settlement of Australia.

THE RACES TO COME
In 1982 ships will gather in Falmouth for the Cutty Sark Tall Ships Race to Lisbon. They will probably be joined for this twenty-first anniversary race by ships from North and South America at the end of an ASTA event. There will follow an exchange of cadets and a cruise in company from Lisbon to Vigo in Spain, with a return race to Southampton. Future events include races from St Malo to Nova Scotia and Quebec in 1984 and to Bremerhaven, Gothenburg and Newcastle in 1986.

The events of the years to come will bring together thousands of competitors from many nations who will sail, if not the Seven Seas, at least thousands of miles, learning to compete amicably and to work together in a friendship that will prove indestructible.

Sail lives on! Karstensens Shipyard, Skagen, building a 26-metre (85-foot) wooden sailing ketch in 1980 for the Swedish Cruising Association (Svenska Kryssarklubbens Seglarskola) at Gothenburg. She is designed to lines from the traditional Brixham trawler, *Gratitude of Gothenburg (Harry Nicolaisen, Göteborgs-Posten)*

APPENDIX A

(Ships taking part in Cutty Sark Tall Ships Races 1980.
Placings in Races One and Two in brackets. Daggers indicate 'retired', asterisks 'disqualified' or 'did not start')

RACE ONE (KIEL TO KARLSKRONA)
CLASS A

Race entered	Name	Nationality	Thames Tonnage	Rig	Hull colour	Sail No	Owners (entered by)	Master
I, II	CREOLE (9 †)	Denmark	699	Staysail Schooner	Black	—	Nyborg Søfartsskole	Bruntse Jorgen
I	DANMARK (6)	Denmark	845	Ship	White	—	Directorate for Maritime Education	Capt Bentsen
I, II	DAR POMORZA (1, 1)	Poland	1784	Ship	White	—	Wyższa Szkoła Morska	Capt T. Olechnowicz
I	GEORG STAGE (5)	Denmark	396	Ship	Black	—	Stiftelsen 'Georg Stages Minde'	Capt B. B. Jespersen
I, II	GORCH FOCK (4, 2)	W. Germany	1727	Barque	White	—	Federal German Navy	Capt Horst Wind
I, II	GUAYAS (2, †)	Ecuador	1097	Barque	White	—	Ecuadorian Navy	Capt Nelson Armas
I, II	KRUZENSHTERN (7, 5)	USSR	3185	Barque	Black	—	Baltic Division of Training Ships	Capt A. B. Perevozchikov
I, II	POGORIA (3, 3)	Poland	314	Barquentine	White	PZ 1980	Iron Shackle Fraternity	Krzysztof Baranowski
I, II	SØRLANDET (8, 4)	Norway	644	Ship	White	—	Town of Kristiansand	Capt Nils Arntsen

Following Class A in Races I and II but not eligible to compete

	SEA CLOUD	W. Germany	2700	Barque	White	—	Tall-Ship Windjammer Sailing Club	Capt H. Paschburg

CLASS B DIVISION I—VESSELS RACING WITHOUT SPINNAKER WITH TCF OF 0.6500 OR LESS

Name	Race entered	Nationality	Thames Tonnage	Rig	Hull colour	Sail no	Owners (entered by)	Master
ALBATROS (14)	I	W. Germany	157	Gaff Schooner	White	TSG 137	Clipper Deutsches Jugendwerk zur See	Heiner Grubmeyer
ANNA ROSA (17)	I	Norway	84	Gaff Ketch	Brown	11	Simrad A/S	Tor Bjerke
ASTARTE (†)	I	W. Germany	84	Gaff Ketch	Black	TSG 126	Schiffergilde Bremerhaven eV	Klaus Walter Rode
ATENE (6)	I	Sweden	92	Gaff Schooner	White	A1	Einar Karlsson	Jens Norregaard
CAROLA (3, 5)	I, II	W. Germany	53	Gaff Ketch	Black	TSG 73	Capt z. S. Hans-Edwin Reith	Capt H-E. Reith
CATARINA (†, ★)	I, II	W. Germany	45	Gaff Ketch	Black	TSG 125	Wolfgang Friederichsen	Wolfgang Friederichsen
CHRISTIANIA (3)	II	Norway	39	Gaff Ketch	White	RS 10	Carl-Emil Petersen	Carl-Emil Petersen
CHRISTIAN VENTURER († 2)	I, II	Bermuda	—	Schooner (Lug)	White	FO 22	Robert R. Doe	Robert R. Doe
COLIN ARCHER (4)	II	Norway	38	Gaff Ketch	White	RS 1	Norsk Sjofartsmuseum	Knut von Trepka
DUSMARIE (12, 6)	I, II	UK	16	Gaff Yawl	Blue	822	Bransons Commonwealth Educational Trust	A. M. Westbury
ELINOR (†, ★)	I, II	Denmark	130	Gaff Schooner	Black	15	Palle Blinkenberg	Palle Blinkenberg
ELLIDA (8)	I	Panama	99	Schooner	Black	8	Harry Freidank	Harry Freidank
EQUINOXE (4, †)	I, II	W. Germany	31	Gaff Cutter	White	TSG 113	Hans-Werner Meyer	Hans-Werner Meyer
GRATIA OF GOTHENBURG (2)	I	Sweden	89	Gaff Ketch	Blue	20	Svenska Kryssarklubbens Seglarskola	Gosta af Klint
GRATITUDE OF GOTHENBURG (1)	I	Sweden	103	Gaff Ketch	Blue	4	Svenska Kryssarklubbens Seglarskola	Kjell Wollter
GRE 14 (†)	II	Holland	34	Gaff Cutter	White/Red	TSH 56	J. Van der Post	J. Van der Post
GRØNLAND (9)	I	W. Germany	87	Gaff Cutter	Black	TSG 117	Deutsches Schiffahrtsmuseum	Manfred Hovener
HOSHI (10, 9)	I, II	UK	50	Gaff Schooner	Green	1887	Island Cruising Club	Peter Masters
JENS KROGH (13, 10)	I, II	Denmark	58	Gaff Ketch	White	TSD 145	FDF/FPF Aalborg Sokreds	Bo Rosbjerg
JOLIE BRISE (5, 8)	I, II	UK	47	Gaff Cutter	Black	DS 2	Exeter Maritime Museum	J. Kapp (I), C. W. Parish (II)
LEDINA (†)	II	Norway	18	Gaff Cutter	White	KR 713	Reidar A. Johansen	Reidar A. Johansen

Div	Ship	Country	No.	Rig	Colour	Code	Operator	Master
I, II	LE PAPILLON (16, †)	USA	34	Gaff Schooner	Green	TSUS 146	Tom Lemm	Tom Lemm
I, II	LINDØ (★★)	USA	176	Topsail Schooner	Black	TSKT 94	Atlantic Schooner Association	G. Francis Birra
II	LIV (1)	Norway	29	Gaff Ketch	White	RS 5	Unni and Arne Smith	Unni Smith
II	MJOJO (see Div II)							
I	OLIFANT (11)	W. Germany	16	Gaff Cutter	Black	TSG 127	Heinrich Woermann	Heinrich Woermann
I, II	OUTLAW (†, 7)	W. Germany	277	Staysail Schooner	Black	TSG 123	Jugendschiff Corsar e V	Peter Schwarz
I, II	RAMROD (see Div III)							
I, II	ROYALIST (7, †)	UK	110	Brig	Black	TSK 23	Sea Cadet Association	Lt-Cdr M. Scott (I) / Cdr D. D. E. Gay (II)
I	SAMPO (15)	Denmark	37	Gaff Ketch	Green	TSD 130	Joergen Hammer	Joergen Hammer
I	SEUTE DEERN (18)	W. Germany	187	Gaff Ketch	Black	TSG 43	Clipper Deutsches Jugendwerk zur See	Peter Lohmeyer
I, II	SVANEN OF STOCKHOLM (13†)	Sweden	61	Staysail Schooner	White	TSS 148	Carl-Magnus Ring	Carl-Magnus Ring

CLASS B DIVISION II—VESSELS RACING WITHOUT SPINNAKER WITH TCF OF 0.6501 OR ABOVE

Race entered	Name	Nationality	Thames Tons	Rig	Hull colour	Sail no	Owners (entered by)	Master
I	AKKA (†)	W. Germany	41	BM Sloop	White	XV 2	Manfred Bessey	Manfred Bessey
I	AMPHITRITE (12)	W. Germany	170	Gaff Schooner	Black	TSG 121	Clipper Deutsches Jugendwerk zur See	Michael v. Gadow
I, II	APOLLO (★★)	Holland	16	BM Ketch	Brown	TSH 158	L. van Gasselt	G. Ulrich
I, II	BELLE POULE (3, 10)	France	275	Topsail Schooner	White	F 30	Marine Nationale	OT 1 Bonniou
II	BELLE VAN ZUYLEN (★)	UK	103	Bermudan Ketch	White	TSH 143	Beaulieu Vessels Limited	G. Baumann
II	BRABANDER (★)	Holland	110	Gaff Schooner	Black/White	TSH 142	F. Franssen	F. Franssen
I, II	CEREOLA (7, †)	UK	19	BM Ketch	White	22	The Hon Greville Howard	H. G. Evans
I	CHWAN (sailed in Div III)	Sweden	20	BM Ketch	Black	756	Jan Andersson	Jan Andersson
I	DIONE (10)	W. Germany	25	BM Ketch	Blue	G 22	Kurt Bambauer	Kurt Bambauer
I, II	DONALD SEARLE (11, 12)	UK	69	BM Ketch	White	TSK 120	The Rona Trust	I. Hinton (I) J. Pearcy (II)
I, II	EENDRACHT (9, 14)	Holland	226	Gaff Schooner	Blue	TSH 47	Netherlands Sail Training Association	H. M. Juta (I) W. P. Jansen (II)
I, II	EL PIRATA (†, †)	UK	128	Gaff Schooner	White	TSK 122	Channel Island Ocean Sailing Association	John Charles Cluett
I, II	ETOILE (2, 2)	France	275	Topsail Schooner	White	F 31	Marine Nationale	Mjr Cousquer
I, II	FALKEN (1, 3)	Sweden	232	Gaff Schooner	White	02	Royal Swedish Navy	R. Westblad
I	FLAMINGO (5)	UK	24	BM Sloop	White	29	British Kiel Yacht Club	Major Gen J. Groom
I, II	HALCYON (8, 7)	UK	78	BM Ketch	White	TSK 23	The College of Nautical Studies	J. H. Kennedy
I, II	JOANA I (†, †)	Canada	38	Gaff Yawl	Black/White	TSKC 129	Antonio Freire/M. T. Perreault	Antonio Freire
II	KANALOA (9)	Holland	16	Bermudan Ketch	White	TSH 134	G. R. Postema	G. R. Postema
I	KRANICH (4)	UK	26	BM Sloop	White	X 7	British Kiel Yacht Club	Lt-Col R. Cemm
II	MALCOLM MILLER (11)	UK	299	Topsail Schooner	Black	TSK 2	STA Schooners	Capt M. Kemmis-Betty

Race entered	Name	Nationality	Thames Tons	Rig	Hull colour	Sail no	Owners (entered by)	Master
II	MASTER BUILDER (13)	UK	50	Bermudan Ketch	White	OYC 3	Ocean Youth Club	Matthew Bowns
II	MJOJO (in Div I) (†)	Holland	24	Gaff Cutter	Blue	TSH 67	P. S. Van Der Post	P. S. Van Der Post
I, II	PETER VON DANZIG (6, 1)	W. Germany	16	Bermudan Sloop	Blue	G 2200	Theobald Schmid/Peter Schmid	Theobald Schmid
II	RAMROD (4)	UK	18	Bermudan Cutter	Blue	144	Colchester Scouts Sailing Scheme	K. Wright
II	RAN (†)	Holland	111	Gaff Schooner	Black	TSH 131	Antony F. de Baat	Antony F. de Baat
II	RAN I (*)	Holland	21	Bermudan Ketch	Yellow	TSH 147	R. A. W. Oomes	R. A. W. Oomes
I, II	SEPHA VOILAARS (†, *)	Holland	166	Gaff Schooner	Black	TSH 34	H. Wever	H. Wever
II	SIR WINSTON CHURCHILL (5)	UK	299	Topsail Schooner	Black	TSK 1	STA Schooners	Capt J. Lawson
II	THE GREAT ESCAPE (8)	Holland	38	Bermudan Ketch	White	TSH 46	Watersport Twellegea	Andries de Groot
I, II	TINA IV (†, *)	W. Germany	54	Bermudan Ketch	White	TSG 81	F. E. Scharfeld	F. E. Scharfeld
II	TINEKE (†)	Holland	16	Bermudan Ketch	Green	TSH 138	W. Twinstra	W. Twinstra
II	ZEW MORZA (*, 6)	Poland	118	Gaff Schooner	White	PZ 2	Polish Yachting Association	T. Puchalczyk
I, II	ZEBU (*, †)	UK	112	Bermudan Ketch	White	–	N. Koller and P. Braggs	P. Hambly

CLASS B DIVISION III—VESSELS RACING WITH SPINNAKERS

Name	Race entered	Nationality	Thames Tons	Rig	Hull colour	Sail no	Owners (entered by)	Master
ATLANTA (†)	I	W. Germany	41	BM Ketch	White	9563	Willi Doden	Berthold Frei
ATHENA (†)	I	W. Germany	32	BM Sloop	White	G 462	Klaus Lower	Ralf Flindt
AVALANCHE (8)	I	UK	27	BM Sloop	White	X 17	Royal Engineer Yacht Club	Major M. W. B. Best
BLANCA ESTELA (7, 4)	I, II	Chile	55	BM Ketch	White	X 159	Chilean Navy	Capt John Martin
BRITISH SOLDIER (†, 2)	I, II	UK	36	BM Cutter	Red	K 684	Joint Services Sailing Centre	Major R. Sjoberg (I) / Lt-Col H. de Fonblanque (II)
CARILLION OF WIGHT (6)	II	UK	24	BM Sloop	Blue	K 296	Christian Sailing Centre	Charles Gladdis
CHWAN (9)	I	Sweden	20	BM Ketch	Black	756	Jan Andersson	Jan Andersson
CREIDNE (†)	II	Ireland	30	BM Ketch	White	TSIR 37	Ministry of Defence, Eire	Len Breewood
DARK HORSE (20, 12)	I, II	UK	50	BM Schooner	White	K1243	Lloyds Bank Limited	T. D. Llewellyn (I) / P. K. Murray (II)
DASHER (†, 1)	I, II	UK	36	BM Cutter	Blue	K1202	Joint Services Sailing Centre	CPO Abrahams (I) / CPO Butcher (II)
DORIS II (13)	II	Poland	22	BM Sloop	Brown	PZ 68	KS Mareton	Lech Laskowski
FREIHERR VON BROMBERG (★)		W. Germany	27	BM Yawl	White	G 50	Rudolf Goebel/ Bruno Leo Kluszczynski	B. L. Kluszczynski
HAJDUK (2, 3)	I, II	Poland	25	BM Sloop	Blue	PZ 808	MKS Pogon	Zygmunt Kowalski (I) / Jerzy Łagiewka (II)
HETMAN (11, 8)	I, II	Poland	31	BM Sloop	Red	PZ 61	Yacht Klub Morski 'Kotwica'	Jan Pinkiewicz
ISIS (12)	I	W. Germany	26	BM Ketch	White	TSG 132	Horst Wiesehahn	Christoph Durr
MEDEA (10)	I	Switzerland	17	BM Sloop	White	TSG 131	Merlens	Rolf Kupper
QUEEN (4)	I	W. Germany	24	BM Sloop	Grey	G1554	K. L. Kohler	Lothar Kohler
RAMROD (19)	I	UK	18	BM Cutter	Blue	144	Colchester Scout Sailing Scheme	Kenneth Wright
RITZA (1, 7)	I, II	USSR	23	BM Sloop	White	2SR 49	Leningrad Marine Engineering College	Capt Antonov
ROZTOCZE (18, 17)	I, II	Poland	39	BM Yawl	Brown	PZ 9	Lublin District Yachting Association	Ziemowit Baranski

	Name	Nationality		Rig	Colour	Sail No.	Owner / Club	Skipper
I, II	SABRE (5, †)	UK	36	BM Yawl	Red	K3178	Joint Services Sailing Centre	Major Humphreys (I) / Major A. Platt (II)
II	SCOTCHMAN (★)	Holland	38	BM Ketch	Blue	TSH 139	Watersport Twellegea	Cees Boersma
II	SCYLLA (★)	Holland	16	BM Ketch	White	TSH 133	Watersport Twellegea	Theo Roeten
I, II	SPARTA (3, 10)	USSR	45	BM Sloop	White	SR 1936	Latvian Shipping Company	Capt A. Chechulin
I	ST BARBARA II (17)	UK	14	BM Sloop	Red	114	Royal Artillery Yacht Club	WO II K. Graham
I, II	STORMVOGEI (★, 15)	Austria	69	BM Ketch	White	700H	Jacek E. Palkiewicz	Jacek E. Palkiewicz
I, II	SYMFONI (21, 14)	Holland	48	BM Ketch	White	TSH 110	Symfoni Charter	Karel Beer
II	TIELSA (†)	Holland	59	BM Ketch	Orange	H 2422	J. Bosma	J.J. Gillissen
I, II	TRYGŁAW (14, 11)	Poland	25	BM Sloop	White	PZ551	Wyzsza Szkoła Morska	Antoni Brancewicz
I, II	URANIA (15, 16)	Holland	65	BM Ketch	White	H 31	Royal Netherlands Navy	Cdr B. Heppener (I) / Lt G. M. Veenman (II)
I, II	WALROSS III (6, 5)	W. Germany	32	BM Sloop	White	G 909	Akademischer Seglar-Verein (Berlin)	Claus Reichardt (I) / Dr A. Schiessler (II)
I, II	WODNIK II (13, 18)	Poland	19	BM Ketch	Brown	PZ926	Zwiazek Harcerstwa Polskiego	Maciej Zarazinski
I, II	WOJEWODA POMORSKI (16, 9)	Poland	45	BM Sloop	Brown	PZ488	Students Yacht Club	Mario Sas Bojarski

APPENDIX B

SPECIFICATIONS OF TALL SHIPS OF THE WORLD (Class A)

Amerigo Vespucci

Country: Italy
Owner: Italian Navy
Rig: Full-rigged ship
Hull colour: Black with two white stripes
Year launched: 1931
Where built: Castellammare di Stabia Shipyard, Italy
Designer: Cdr (Eng) Francesco Rotundi
Original owners: Italian Navy
Displacement: 4,100 tons
Thames tonnage: 1,500 tons
Length overall: 100 metres (328 feet)
Length waterline: 70 metres (230 feet)
Beam: 15.6 metres (51 feet)
Draught: 7 metres (23 feet)
Mainmast height above deck: 46.6 metres (153 feet)
Mainmast height above waterline: 51 metres (167 feet)
Sail area: approximately 3,000 square metres
Auxiliary power: 2,000 hp
Total complement: 450
Officers: 25 **Crew:** 275 **Cadets:** 150
Commanding officer 1980: Captain G. Iannucci
Motto: '*Non Chi Comincia ma quel che Persevera*'—'Not he who just starts, but he who perseveres to fulfil his task' (attributed to Leonardo da Vinci)

Christian Radich

Country: Norway
Owner: Østlandets Skoleskib
Rig: Full-rigged ship
Hull colour: White
Year launched: 1937
Where built: Framnes Mekaniske Verksted, Sandefjord, Norway
Designer: Captain Chr Blom
Original owners: Østlandets Skoleskib
Gross registered tonnage: 676 tons
Thames tonnage: 773 tons
Length overall: 62.5 metres (205 feet)
Length overall (with bowsprit): 73.15 metres (240 feet)
Length waterline: 53 metres (174 feet)
Beam: 9.7 metres (32 feet)
Draught: 4.5 metres (15 feet)
Mainmast height above water: 39 metres (128 feet)
Sail area: 1,350 square metres
Auxiliary power: 650 hp
Total complement: 102
Officers: 14 **Cadets:** 88
Master 1973–8: Captain Kjell Thorsen
Master 1978–80: Captain Jan Fjeld Hansen

Creole

Country: Denmark
Owner: Nyborg Søfartsskole, Denmark
Rig: Three-masted staysail schooner
Hull colour: Black
Year launched: 1927
Where built: Camper and Nicholson's, Gosport
Designer: C. E. Nicholson
Original name: *Vira*
Thames tonnage: 699 tons
Length overall: 58 metres (190 feet)
Beam: 9.45 metres (31 feet)
Draught: 4.69 metres (15½ feet)
Mainmast height above deck: 41.3 metres (135 feet)
Sail area: STA rated, 975 square metres in 1980
Total complement: 48
Officers: 7 **Crew:** 4 **Trainees:** 37
Master in 1980: Bruntse Jorgen

Danmark

Country: Denmark
Owner: Directorate for Maritime Education, Denmark
Rig: Full-rigged ship

Hull colour: White
Year launched: 1933
Designer: Aage Larsen
Where built: Nakskov Shipyard, Denmark
Original owners: Directorate for Maritime Education, Copenhagen, Denmark
Gross registered tonnage: 790 tons
Thames tonnage: 845 tons
Length overall (with bowsprit):
77.1 metres (253 feet)
Length overall: 64.7 metres (213 feet)
Length waterline: 60.3 metres (198 feet)
Beam: 10 metres (33 feet)
Draught: 5.2 metres (17 feet)
Mainmast height above waterline:
39.6 metres (130 feet)
Sail area: 1,636 square metres
Length of main yard: 20.1 metres (66 feet)
Total length standing wire rigging:
2,005 metres (6,580 feet)
Total length of running wire rigging:
3,700 metres (12,130 feet)
Total length of running ropes: 8,000 metres (26,230 feet)
Auxiliary power: 486 hp
Total complement: 100 (all male)
Officers: 20 **Cadets:** 80 (boys only)
Master in 1980 from January to July:
Captain Wilhelm Hansen
Master in 1980 from July to December:
Captain Otto L. Bentsen

Dar Pomorza

Country: Poland
Owner: Wyższa Szkoła Morska (Merchant Navy Academy), Gdynia, Poland
Rig: Full-rigged ship
Hull colour: White
Year launched: 1909
Where built: Blohm and Voss, Hamburg
Designers: Blohm and Voss
Original owners: Deutscher Schulschiff Verein
Original names:
  Prinzess Eitel Friedrich
  Colbert
  Pomorze (1929)
  Dar Pomorza (1930)
Gross registered tonnage: 1,561 tons
Thames tonnage: 1,784 tons
Length (with bowsprit): 91 metres (299 feet)
Length waterline: 72.6 metres (238 feet)
Beam: 12.6 metres (41 feet)

Draught: 5.7 metres (18½ feet)
Mainmast height above water:
44 metres (144 feet)
Sail area: 2,200 square metres
Auxiliary power: 430 hp
Total complement: 168 (all male)
Officers: 16 **Crew:** 23 **Cadets:** 129
Master in 1980: Captain Tadeusz Olechnowicz
Awards: Cutty Sark Trophy (1980)
Since 1929 she has been commanded by the following Extra-Masters:

1929–38	Konstanty Maciejewicz
1938–9	Konstanty Kowalski
1939–45	Alojzy Kwiatkowski
1945–6	Zbigniew Zebrowski
1946–53	Stefan Gorazdowski
1953–77	Kazimierz Jurkiewicz
1977–	Tadeusz Olechnowicz

Eagle

Owner: United States Coast Guard Academy
Country: United States of America
Hull colour: White, with distinctive red band on bow
Rig: Three-masted barque
Length overall: 82 metres (266 feet)
Beam: 12 metres (39 feet)
Draught: 4.8 metres (16 feet)
Tonnage: 1,634 tons displacement
Thames tonnage: 1,727 tons
Year built: 1936
Where built: Blohm and Voss, Hamburg
Original owners: German Navy
Original name: *Horst Wessel*
Total complement: 189
Officers: 14 **Crew:** 40 **Cadets:** 135

Esmeralda

Owner: Chilean Navy
Country: Chile
Hull colour: White
Rig: Four-masted barquentine
Length overall: 94.8 metres (309 feet)
Length (with bowsprit): 112.8 metres (370 feet)
Beam: 13.11 metres (43 feet)
Tonnage: 3,222 tons displacement
Thames tonnage: 2,478 tons
Year built: 1952
Where built: Echevarrieta y Larringa, Cadiz
Original owners: Chilean Navy

Total complement: 336
Officers: 18 **Crew:** 148 **Cadets:** 170

Georg Stage

Country: Denmark
Owner: Stiftelsen 'Georg Stages Minde'
Rig: Full-rigged ship
Hull colour: Black
Year launched: 1935
Where built: Frederikshavn Vaerft, Denmark
Original owners: Stiftelsen, 'Georg Stages Minde'
Gross registered tonnage: 298 tons
Thames tonnage: 396 tons
Length overall: 45.7 metes (151 feet)
Length waterline: 37.7 metres (124 feet)
Beam: 8.5 metres (28 feet)
Draught: 4 metres (13 feet)
Mainmast height above deck: 28 metres (92 feet)
Sail area: 859 square metres
Auxiliary power: 200 hp
Total complement: 70 (all male)
Officers: 10 **Cadets:** 60 (boys only)
Usual age range of cadets: 16–20
Master in 1980: Captain B. Barner Jespersen

Gloria

Country: Colombia
Owner: Colombian Navy
Hull colour: White
Rig: Three-masted barque
Length overall: 76 metres (249 feet)
Beam: 10.5 metres (34¾ feet)
Draught: 4.35 metres (14¼ feet)
Thames tonnage: 1,097 tons
Year built: 1968
Where built: Astilleros Talleres Celaya SA, Bilbao, Spain
Original owners: Colombian Navy
Total complement: 145
Officers: 20 **Permanent crew:** 65
Cadets: 60

Gorch Fock II

Country: West Germany
Owner: Federal German Navy
Rig: Three-masted barque
Hull colour: White
Year built: 1958
Where built: Blohm and Voss, Hamburg
Original owners: Federal German Navy

Gross registered tonnage: 1,740 tons
Thames tonnage: 1,727 tons
Length overall: 81 metres (266 feet)
Length (with bowsprit): 90 metres (295 feet)
Length waterline: 68.3 metres (224 feet)
Beam: 12 metres (39 feet)
Draught: 4.75 metres (15½ feet)
Mainmast height above waterline: 46 metres (149 feet)
Auxiliary power: 800 hp
Total complement: 198
Officers: 13 **Crew:** 65 **Cadets:** 120
Commanding Officer in 1980: Captain Horst Wind

Guayas

Country: Ecuador
Owner: Ecuadorian Navy
Rig: Three-masted barque
Hull colour: White
Year launched: 1977
Where built: Astilleros Talleres Celaya, SA, Bilbao, Spain
Original owners: Ecuadorian Navy
Gross registered tonnage: 1,153 tons
Thames tonnage: 1,097 tons
Length overall: 78.4 metres (257 feet)
Length waterline: 61.4 metres (200 feet)
Beam: 10.26 metres (33½ feet)
Draught: 4.7 metres (15 feet)
Mainmast height above waterline: 41.9 metres (137 feet)
Total complement: 150
Officers: 20 **Crew:** 30 **Trainees:** 100
Commanding Officer in 1980: Captain Nelson Armas
Awards: ASTA Cutty Sark Friendship Trophy (1980)

Juan Sebastian de Elcano

Country: Spain
Owner: Spanish Navy
Hull colour: White
Rig: Four-masted topsail schooner
Length overall: 94.8 metres (309 feet)
LOA (with bowsprit): 112.8 metres (370 feet)
Beam: 13.11 metres (43 feet)
Draught: 8.7 metres (28½ feet)
Tonnage: 3,222 tons displacement
Thames tonnage: 2,478 tons
Mainmast height above water: 52 metres (170 feet)

Year built: 1927
Where built: Echevarrieta y Larringa
Original owners: Spanish Navy
Total complement: 410
Officers: 24   **Crew:** 176   **Cadets:** 210

Kruzenshtern

Country: USSR
Owner: Trawl Fleet of Riga, Western Division of Training Vessels, Ministry of Fisheries of the USSR
Rig: Four-masted barque
Hull colour: Black with a white stripe
Year built: 1926
Where built: J. C. Tecklenborg, Bremerhaven-Geestemünde
Original owners: F. Laeisz ('P' Line), Hamburg
Original name: *Padua*
Gross registered tonnage: 3,064 tons
Thames tonnage: 3,185 tons
Length overall (with bowsprit): 114.5 metres (376 feet)
Length waterline: 95.5 metres ($313\frac{1}{3}$ feet)
Beam: 14.02 metres (46 feet)
Draught: 6.85 metres ($22\frac{1}{2}$ feet)
Mainmast height, above deck: 52 metres ($170\frac{1}{2}$ feet)
Mainmast height, above water: 56 metres ($183\frac{1}{2}$ feet)
Sail area: 3,656 square metres
Auxiliary power: Two engines of 800 hp each
Total complement: 270
Officers: 24   **Crew:** 71   **Cadets:** on average, 175 (all male)
Usual age range of cadets: 18–20
Master in 1980: Captain Alexey Perevozchikov
Awards: Cutty Sark Trophy (1974)

Pogoria

Country: Poland
Owner: Iron Shackle Fraternity (Polish television)
Rig: Barquentine
Hull colour: White with blue stripe
Year built: 1980
Where built: Gdansk Shipyard
Designer: Zygmunt Choreń
Original owners: Iron Shackle Fraternity
Displacement: 342 tons
Thames tonnage: 314 tons
Length overall: 47 metres (154 feet)

Beam: 8 metres (26 feet)
Draught: 3.5 metres ($11\frac{1}{2}$ feet)
Mainmast height above deck: 29.4 metres ($96\frac{1}{2}$ feet)
Mainmast height above water: 31.56 metres ($103\frac{1}{2}$ feet)
Auxiliary power: 310 hp
Total complement: 56
Officers: 15   **Crew:** 5   **Trainees:** 36
Master in 1980: Krzysztof Baranowski

Sagres II

Country: Portugal
Owner: Portuguese Navy (since 1961)
Hull colour: White
Rig: Three-masted barque
Length overall: 80.58 metres ($267\frac{1}{2}$ feet)
Beam: 12 metres ($39\frac{1}{2}$ feet)
Draught: 5.25 metres ($17\frac{1}{4}$ feet)
Thames tonnage: 1,784 tons
Year built: 1937
Where built: Blohm and Voss, Hamburg
Original owners: German Navy
Original names: *Albert Leo Schlageter*
Guanabara (Brazilian Navy)
Total complement: 203
Officers: 9   **Crew:** 90   **Cadets:** 104

Sea Cloud

Country: West Germany (registered in Grand Cayman)
Owner: Tall-Ship (Windjammer) Sailing Club Ltd, Hamburg, West Germany
Rig: Four-masted barque
Hull colour: White
Year launched: 1931
Where built: Germania Shipyard, Kiel
Original owner: Marjorie Hutton
Original names: *Hussar,* later *Sea Cloud,* then *Angelita, Patria, Antarna*
Displacement: 3,530 tons
Thames tonnage: 2,700 tons
Length overall: 107.5 metres (353 feet)
Length waterline: 77.2 metres ($253\frac{1}{4}$ feet)
Beam: 14.9 metres (49 feet)
Draught: 5 metres (16 feet)
Mainmast height above deck: 58.4 metres ($191\frac{1}{2}$ feet)
Sail area: 3,160 square metres
Auxiliary power: 6,000 bhp
Total complement: 90 during races, 135 approximate maximum
Trainees: 25 (during races)

Sedov

Country: USSR
Owner: Baltic Division of Training Ships of the Fisheries Service of the USSR
Hull colour: Black with white stripe
Rig: Four-masted barque
LOA: 117.65 metres (386 feet)
Beam: 14.63 metres (48 feet)
Depth in hold: 8.08 metres (26 feet 7 inches)
Tonnage:
    3,476 tons gross
    5,300 tons displacement
Mainmast height above deck: 54.5 metres (178 feet 10 inches)
Length of mainyard: 30.4 metres (99$\frac{3}{4}$ feet)
Length of royal yard: 14.48 metres (47$\frac{1}{2}$ feet)
Number of sails: 34
Year built: 1921
Where built: Germania Werft (Friedrich Krupp), Kiel, Germany
Original owners: F. A. Vinnen, Bremen
Original name: *Magdalene Vinnen II* (later) *Kommodore Johnsen* (1936)

Sørlandet

Country: Norway
Owner: The town and population of Kristiansand
Rig: Full-rigged ship
Hull colour: White
Year launched: 1927
Where built: P. Høivolds Mek Verksted, Kristiansand
Designer: E. Vik
Original owner: Sørlandets Seilende Skoleskibs Institution
Gross registered tonnage: 568 tons
Thames tonnage: 644 tons
Length overall: 57 metres (186 feet)
Length waterline: 48.16 metres (158 feet)
Beam: 8.87 metres (29 feet)
Draught: 4.27 metres (14 feet)
Mainmast height above waterline: 35.05 metres (115 feet)
Sail area: 1,166 square metres (maximum possible)
Auxiliary power: 564 hp
Total complement: 84
Officers: 6   **Crew:** 8   **Cadets:** 70
Master in 1980: Captain Nils Arntsen
Master 1956–64: Captain Paul Hegstrøm
Master 1964–74: Captain Nils Arntsen

FURTHER CLASS A SHIPS IN COMMISSION IN THE WORLD

Captain Miranda

Country: Uruguay
Owner: Uruguayan Navy
Rig: Three-masted schooner
Built: 1930
Tonnage: 600 tons displacement
Total complement: 85
Recommissioned in 1977–8 as a naval sailing schoolship

Libertad

Country: Argentina
Owner: Argentine Navy
Year built: 1956
Thames tonnage: 2,587 tons
Rig: Ship
Total complement: 365

Mircea

Country: Romania
Owner: Merchant Marine Nautical College, Romania
Year built: 1939
Rig: Three-masted barque
Thames tonnage: 1,727 tons
Built for present owners by Blohm and Voss
Sistership to *Tovarisch, Sagres II* and *Eagle*

Nippon Maru and Kaiwa Maru

Country: Japan
Owner: Ministry of Transport, Japan
Year built: 1930
Built for: Present owners
Rig: Four-masted barques—sister ships
Gross tonnage: 2,250 tons

Tovarisch

Country: USSR
Owner: Kherson Marine School, USSR
Year built: 1933
Built for: German Navy
Builders: Blohm and Voss, Hamburg
Rig: Three-masted barque
Thames tonnage: 1,727 tons
Total complement: 190
Original owners: German Navy
Original name: *Gorch Fock*

APPENDIX C

TALL SHIPS RACES 1956–79: FIRST AND SECOND PRIZE WINNERS

Torbay to Lisbon, 1956
Class I
First: *Moyana*, UK; *second: Christian Radich*, Norway
Class II
First: *Artica II*, Italy; *second: Juana*, Argentina

Brest to Las Palmas, 1958
Class I
First: *Sagres*, Portugal; *second: Christian Radich*, Norway
Class II
First: *L'Etoile*, France; *second: Belle Poule*, France
Class III
First: *Artica II*, Italy; *second: Sereine*, France

Brest to La Coruña, 1958
Class II
First: *Myth of Malham*, UK; *second: Marie Christine II*, France

Cannes to Naples, 1960
Class I
First: *Gorch Fock*, W. Germany; *second: Verona*, UK
Class II
First: *Belle Aventure*, Monaco; *second: Altair*, Argentina

Oslo to Ostend, 1960
Class I
First: *Statsraad Lehmkuhl*, Norway; *second: Sørlandet*, Norway
Class II
First: *Nordwind*, UK; *second: Wyvern*, Norway
Class III
First: *Lutine*, UK; *second: Merlin*, UK

Torbay to Rotterdam, 1962
Class I
First: *Gorch Fock*, W. Germany; *second: Sørlandet*, Norway
Class II
First: *Corsaro II*, Italy; *second: Wyvern*, Norway

Class III
First: *Glénan*, France; *second, Wishstream*, UK

Plymouth to Lisbon, 1964
Class II A
First: *Belle Poule*, France; *second: L'Etoile*, France
Class II B
First: *Tawau*, UK; *second: Hoshi*, UK
Class III
First: *Bloodhound*, UK; *second: Lutine*, UK

Lisbon to Bermuda, 1964
Class I
First: *Christian Radich*, Norway; *second: Danmark*, Denmark
Class II
First: *Corsaro II*, Italy; *second: Tawau*, UK
Class III
First: *Peter von Danzig*, W. Germany; *second: Merlin*, UK

Southsea to Cherbourg, 1965
Class B
First: *Urania*, Netherlands; *second: Rona*, UK
Class C
First: *Lily Maid*, UK; *second: Griffin II*, UK

Falmouth to the Skaw, 1966
Class A
First: *Sørlandet*, Norway; *second: Christian Radich*, Norway
Class B I
First: *Sir Winston Churchill*, UK; *second: Falken*, Sweden
Class B II
First: *Centurion*, UK; *second: Duet*, UK
Class C I
First: *Zulu*, UK; *second: Lutine*, UK
Class C II
First: *Sereine*, France; *second: Galahad*, UK

Skaw to Den Helder, 1966
Class A
First: *Gorch Fock*, W. Germany

Class B
First: Urania, Netherlands; second: Sir Winston Churchill, UK
Class C
First: Najade, Netherlands; second: Merlin, UK

Southsea to Cherbourg, 1966
Class B
First: Rona, UK; second: Halcyon, UK
Class C
First: Merlin, UK; second: Griffin II, UK

Southsea to Cherbourg, 1967
Class B
First: Duet, UK; second: Rona, UK
Class C
First: Griffin III, UK; second: Wishstream, UK

Gothenburg to Kristiansand, 1968
Class A
First: Gorch Fock, W. Germany; second: Sørlandet, Norway
Class B
First: Gladan, Sweden; second: Falken, Sweden

Harwich to Kristiansand, 1968
Class B
First: Rona, UK; second: Duet, UK
Class C I
First: Zulu, UK; second: Kaylena, UK
Class C II
First: Gawaine, UK; second: Martlet, UK

Kristiansand to Southsea, 1968
Class I
First: Lutine, UK; second: Kaylena, UK
Class II
First: Zulu, UK; second: Iroise, France

Portsmouth to Cherbourg, 1968
Class B
First: Malcolm Miller, UK; second: Theodora, UK
Class C
First: Griffin III, UK; second: Aloha of Hamble, UK

Southsea to Cherbourg, 1969
Class I
First: Urania, Netherlands; second: Asgard, Eire

Class II
First: Griffin III, UK; second: Merlin, UK

Weymouth to St Malo, 1969
Class I
First: Halcyon, UK; second: Robert Gordon, UK
Class II
First: Corabia, Netherlands; second: Peter von Danzig, W. Germany

Plymouth to Tenerife, 1970
Class A
First: Christian Radich, Norway; second: Statsraad Lehmkuhl, Norway
Class B I
First: Stella Polare, Italy; second: Falken, Sweden
Class B II
First: Najade, Netherlands; second: Zulu, UK

Plymouth to La Coruña, 1970
Class B I
First: Hoshi, UK; second: Provident, UK
Class B II
First: Martlet, UK; second: Gauntlet, UK

Weymouth to St Malo, 1970
Class B
First: Urania, Netherlands; second: Rampage, UK

Southsea to Cherbourg, 1970
Class B I
First: Asgard, Eire; second: Merlin, UK
Class B II
First: Rampage, UK; second: Sakr el Bahr, UK

Monaco to Porto Cervo, 1971
Class B
First: La Belle Poule, France; second: L'Etoile, France

Porto Cervo to Malta, 1971
Class B
First: La Belle Poule, France; second: Rampage, UK

Southsea to Cherbourg, 1971
Class B II
First: Asgard, Eire; second: Merlin, UK

Weymouth to St Malo, 1971
Class B I
First: Asgard, Eire; *second: Robert Gordon*, UK
Class B II
First: Malcolm Miller, UK; *second: Halcyon*, UK

The Solent to the Skaw, 1972
Class A
First: Dar Pomorza, Poland; *second: Gorch Fock*, West Germany
Class B I
First: Sir Winston Churchill, UK; *second: Malcolm Miller*, UK
Class B II
First: Rona, UK; *second: Acteon*, UK
Class B III
First: Gryphis, UK; *second: Zulu*, UK

Heligoland to Dover, 1972
Class B I
First: Cynara, UK; *second: Falken*, Sweden
Class B II
First: Asgard, Eire; *second: Zulu*, UK

Helsinki to Falsterbo, 1972
Class A
First: Christian Radich, Norway; *second: Danmark*, Denmark
Class B I
First: Gladan, Sweden; *second: Falken*, Sweden
Class B II
First: Asta, W. Germany; *second: St Barbara II*, UK

Weymouth to St Malo, 1972
Class B
First: Sailing Swiss, Switzerland; *second: White Knight*, UK

Southsea to Cherbourg, 1972
Class B
First: Falmouth Packet, UK; *second: Marabu*, UK

Weymouth to St Malo, 1973
Class B I
First: Dodo IV, UK; *second: Malcolm Miller*, UK
Class B II
First: Midship-Ca, France; *second: Pen-ar-Vir*, France

Southsea to Cherbourg, 1973
Class B
First: Sabre, UK; *second: Samuel Whitbread*, UK

Southsea to Cherbourg, August 1973
Class B I
First: Dodo IV, UK; *second: Urania*, Netherlands
Class B II
First: Kyrah, Switzerland; *second: Sailing Swiss*, Switzerland

Dartmouth to La Coruña, 1974
Class B I (vessels above 30 tons)
First: Sabre, UK; *second: Adventure*, UK
Class B II (vessels 30 tons and below)
First: Marabu, UK; *second: Sovereign*, France

Copenhagen to Gdynia, 1974
Class A
First: Tovarisch, USSR; *second: Gorch Fock*, W. Germany
Class B I (vessels 50 tons and above)
First: America, USA; *second: Thyra*, Denmark
Class B II (vessels below 50 tons TM)
First: Karin, W. Germany; *second: Evaine*, UK

La Coruña to Portsmouth, 1974
Class B I (vessels of 50 tons and over)
First: Stella Polare, Italy; *second: Sir Winston Churchill*, UK
Class B II (vessels of less than 50 tons)
First: Glénan, France; *second: Sabre*, UK

St Malo to the Nab Tower (Portsmouth), 1974
Class B I (vessels above 50 tons)
First: La Belle Poule, France; *second: Malcolm Miller*, UK
Class B II (vessels 50 tons and under)
First: Vanity, Switzerland; *second: Sovereign*, France

IJmuiden to Den Helder, 1975
Class B I (vessels 50 tons and over)
First: Falken, Sweden; *second: Gladan*, Sweden
Class B II (vessels under 50 tons)
First: Zulu, UK; *second: Fanfare of Essex*, UK

Den Helder to the Thames Estuary, 1975
Class B I (vessels 50 tons and over)
First: Falken, Sweden; *second: Urania*,
Netherlands
Class B II (vessels under 50 tons)
First: Barbican, UK; *second: Fanfare of Essex*,
UK

Southsea to Cherbourg, 1975
Class B I
First: Master Builder, UK; *second: Halcyon*, UK
Class B II
First: Uomie, UK; *second: Rampion*, UK

**Plymouth to Santa Cruz de Tenerife,
1976**
Class A
First: Tovarisch, USSR; *second: Kruzenshtern*,
USSR
Class B I
First: Sir Winston Churchill, UK; *second:
Gladan*, Sweden
Class B II
First: Tenerife, Spain; *second: Glénan*, France

**Santa Cruz de Tenerife to Bermuda,
1976**
Class A
First: Tovarisch, USSR; *second: Kruzenshtern*,
USSR
Class B I
First: Gipsy Moth V, UK; *second: Gladan*,
Sweden
Class B II
First: Stella Polare, Italy; *second: Stortebeker*,
W. Germany

**Bermuda to Newport, Rhode Island,
1976**
Class A
First: Gorch Fock, W. Germany; *second: Dar
Pomorza*, Poland
Class B I
First: Ticonderoga, USA; *second: Escapade*,
USA
Class B II
First: Olinka, USA; *second: Hetman*, Poland

Boston to Plymouth, 1976
Class A
First: Phoenix, Eire

Class B I
First: Gipsy Moth V, UK; *second: Gladan*,
Sweden
Class B II
First: Sabre, UK; *second: Kukri*, UK

Isle of Wight to Le Havre, 1977
Class B I
First: Gladan, Sweden; *second: Falken*, Sweden
Class B II
First: Electron of Portsea, UK; *second: Lutine*,
UK

Gothenburg to Oslo, 1978
Class A
First: Gorch Fock, W. Germany; *second:
Christian Radich*, Norway
Class B I
First: Gratitude, Sweden; *second: Leader*,
Sweden
Class B II
First: Sunlight, Norway; *second: Ritza*, USSR

Great Yarmouth to Oslo, 1978
Class B I
First: Duet, UK; *second: Jolie Brise*, UK
Class B II
First: Wyvern, UK; *second: Chaser*, UK

Oslo to Harwich, 1978
Class A
First: Kruzenshtern, USSR; *second: Marques*,
UK
Class B I
First: Sir Winston Churchill, UK; *second,
Dusmarie*, UK
Class B II
First: Chaser, UK; *second: Kukri*, UK

Fowey to the Isle of Man, 1979
Class B I
First: Rona, UK; *second: America*, USA
Class B II
First: Dasher, UK; *second: Adventure*, UK

Round the Isle of Man, 1979
Class B I
First: America, USA; *second: Rona*, UK
Class B II
First: Carillion of Wight, UK; *second: Sabre*,
UK

BIBLIOGRAPHY

Books published in the United Kingdom
Admiralty charts and publications
Ansted., A, *Dictionary of Sea Terms* (Brown, Son and Ferguson, 1st edition, 1920)
Atkinson, Jenni, *A Girl in Square-Rig* (Arlington Books, 1977); reissued in paperback by Arrow under the title *A Girl before the Mast* (1979)
Beken, Frank and Keith, *Beken of Cowes, 1897–1914* (Cassell, 1966)
Beken, Keith, *The Beken File* (Channel Press, 1980)
Berlitz European Phrase Book (Berlitz, Switzerland, 1974)
Binns, Alan, *Viking Voyagers* (Heinemann, 1980)
Burgess, F. H., *A Dictionary of Sailing* (Penguin, 1961)
Carr, Frank G. G., *The Cutty Sark* (Pitkin Pictorial, 1976)
Carse, Robert, *Twilight of Sailing Ships* (Harrap, 1965)
Corin, John, *Provident and the Story of the Brixham Smacks* (Tops'l Books, 1980)
Drummond, Maldwin, *Tall Ships, The World of Sail Training* (Angus & Robertson, 1976)
Falconer's Marine Dictionary (first published by T. Cadell, 1769, reprinted by David & Charles, 1970)
Feversham, Lord, *Great Yachts* (Anthony Blond, 1970)
Fodor's Guide to Scandinavia (Hodder & Stoughton, 1980)
Francis, Clare, *Come Wind or Weather* (Pelham Books, 1978, Sphere, 1979)
Gordon, William, and Lauder, Hugh, *Windjammers* (Collins, 1938)
Hambly, Peter, *Race Under Sail* (Stanford Maritime, 1978)
Hansen, Hans Jurgen, and Benno Wundshammer, *Windjammer Parade* (Ian Allen, 1972)
Hugill, Stan, *Shanties and Sailors' Songs* (Herbert Jenkins, 1969)
—, —, *Shanties from Seven Seas* (Routledge, 1961)
—, —, *Songs of the Sea* (McGraw-Hill, 1977)
Hugo's Scandinavian Phrase Book (Hugo, 1970)
Hurst, A. A., *The Sailing Schoolships* (Hemmel Locke, 1962)
—, —, *Square-Riggers: The Final Epoch* (Teredo Books, 1972)
Hutson, Tony, *Your Book of Tall Ships* (Faber, 1978)
Illingworth, John H., *The Malham Story* (Nautical Publishing Co, 1972)
—, —, *Offshore* (Adlard Coles, 1963)
—, —, *Further Offshore* (Adlard Coles, 1969)

Kemp, Peter (ed), *The Oxford Companion to Ships and the Sea* (Oxford University Press, 1976)

Knox-Johnston, Robin, *Twilight of Sail* (Sidgwick & Jackson, 1978)

Leather, John, *Colin Archer and the Seaworthy Double-ender* (Stanford Maritime, 1979)

—, —, and Smith, Roger M., *Panorama of Gaff Rig* (Barrie & Jenkins, 1977)

Lloyd's Registers (various)

Longman's English Larousse (Longman, 1968)

McGowan, Captain Gordon, USCG (Retd), *The Skipper and the Eagle* (Van Nostrand Reinhold, 1977)

March, Edgar, J., *Sailing Trawlers* (1st edition, Percival Marshall, 1953; 2nd edition, David & Charles, 1970)

Marriner, John, *Afloat in Europe* (Adlard Coles, 1967)

Muir's Historical Atlas (George Philip & Son, 1969)

Nordbok, A. B., *Lore of Ships, The* (1st edition in Swedish, Gothenburg, 1975; English translation, Nordbok, 1978)

Popescu, Julian, *Let's Visit Poland* (Burke, 1979)

Reed, Thomas, *Reed's Nautical Almanac* (Reed, 1981)

Rees, Gareth, *Tall Ships* (Phaidon, 1978)

Sailing (Chatto & Windus, 1935)

Schauffelen, Otmar, *Great Sailing Ships* (Adlard Coles, 1969)

Tall Ships, The, A Sailing Celebration (Patrick Stephens, 1977)

Underhill, Harold A., *Sail Training and Cadet Ships* (Brown, Son & Ferguson, 1956)

Villiers, Alan, *Falmouth for Orders* (Geoffrey Bles, 1929)

—, —, *Cruise of the Conrad* (1st edition, Hodder & Stoughton, 1937; 2nd edition, Pan, 1956; 2nd revised edition, Pan, 1973)

—, —, *Making of a Sailor* (George Routledge, 1938)

—, —, *Way of a Ship* (Hodder & Stoughton, 1954)

—, —, *Sailing Eagle* (Scribner & Sons, New York, 1955)

—, —, *Give Me a Ship to Sail* (Hodder & Stoughton, 1958)

—, —, *War with Cape Horn* (Hodder & Stoughton, 1971)

—, —, *Voyaging with the Wind* (National Maritime Museum, HMSO, 1975)

Winchester, Clarence (ed), *Shipping Wonders of the World* (Amalgamated Press, 1938)

Books published abroad
Denmark

Bygholm, Henrik, Haagen, Peter, Kirkegaard, Carl Aage, and Steen, Peter, *All Sails Set: Ships around a Sail Training Race* (Bygholm, Frederikshavn, 1981; dual Anglo-Danish text)

Lund, Kaj, *Training Vessels under Sail* (Skandinavisk Bogforlag A/S, Odense, 1969; available in English)

—, —, *The Sail Training Ship*

Simonsen, Jørgen D., *Maend af Drenge* (Lademann, Copenhagen, 1976)

Holland

Beukema, Hans, *Sail Ahoy* (published in association with Sail Amsterdam, 1980, by De Boer Maritiem)

Huitema, Dr T., *Ronde en Platbodem Jachten* (P. N. van Kampen & Zoon, BV, 1977)

Veenman, Lieutenant G., RNLN, *The History of H M Nl S Urania* (to be published)

Italy

Ghetti, Mazzucco, and Pucciarelli, Curzio, *Amerigo Vespucci e i secoli d'oro della vela* (Libreria Editrice Frattina, Rome, 1971)

Palkiewicz, Jacek E., *Beyond Any Limits* (Mursia, Milan)

—, —, *The Last Mohican of the Oceans*

Japan

Nakamura, Tsuneo, *Wind and Sail* (Obunsha Publishing Co)

—, —, *The Tall Ships of the World, I* (Heibonsha Publishing Co)

—, —, *The Tall Ships of the World, II* (Heibonsha Publishing Co)

—, —, *The Tall Ships* (Asahi-Sonorama)

—, —, *The Tall Ships: Nippon Maru and Kaiwo Maru* (Rippu Publishing Co)

—, —, *The Tall Ship: Kaiwo Maru* (Kodansha Publishing Co)

Norway

Thorsen, Captain Kjell, *Christian Radich: The Adventure of Oslo's Square-Rigger* (J. W. Cappelens Forlag A/S, 1977; translated into English by Lizann Disch, 1980)

Poland

Baranowski, Krzysztof, *Wyscig do Newport* (1976)

—, —, *Polonez* (1977; available in English)

—, —, *Żaglem Po Ameryce* (1978)

—, —, *Dom Pod Zglami* (1980)

Kabat, Henryk, *Dar Pomorza* (Wydawnictwo Morskie, Gdansk, 1974; available in English)

Meissner, Tadeusz, *Dookoła świata na 'Darze Pomorza'* (Lwów–Warszawa, 1936)

Miazgowski, Boleław, *'Dar Pomorza'* (Sport i Turystyka, Warsaw, 1959)

Murawska, Grażyna, *Operacja Żagiel, 1972* (Wydawnictwo Morskie, Gdansk, 1974)

—, —, *Operacja Żagiel, 1974* (Wydawnictwo Morskie, Gdansk, 1975)

Perepeczko, Andrzej. *Biała Fregata* (Wydawnictwo Morskie, Gdansk, 1974)

—, —, *Dar Pomorza* (Wydawnictwo Morskie, Gdansk, 1974)

Urbanyi, Zbigniew, *Od Daru Pomorza do Ziemi Bydgoskiej* (Wydawnictwo Morskie, Gdansk, 1973)

Sweden

Dahl, Claes-Göran, *Sail Karlskrona* (Axel Abrahamsons, Tryckeriaktiebolag, Karlskrona, 1980; dual Anglo/Swedish text)

Karlskrona, 300 Ar, 1680–1980, Karlskrona Kommun (Torkel Lindeberg, Stockholm, 1979; available in English)

Nordbok, A. B. *et al, Lore of Ships* (Gothenburg, 1975; Swedish and English editions)

A Record of the 300th Anniversary Celebrations (1980)

United States of America

McGowan, Captain Gordon, USCG (Retd), *The Skipper and the Eagle* (Van Nostrand Reinhold, New York, 1977)

Norton, William I., *Eagle Ventures* (M. Evans, New York, 1969)

Regan, Paul M., and Johnson, Paul H., *Eagle Seamanship—A Manual for Square-Rigger Sailing* (Naval Institute Press, Annapolis, Maryland, 1979; revised edition). Previous edition written for the United States Coast Guard Academy by William I. Norton (M. Evans, New York, 1969)

Tall Ships Pacific (American Sail Training Association/Rand McNally, 1978)

Tall Ships, 1976 (Cruising World Publications, 1976)

Windjammer: The Story of Louis de Rochemont's Windjammer, A Modern Adventure in Cinemiracle, featuring the *Christian Radich* (Random House, Inc, 1958)

West Germany

Hansen, Hans Jurgen, and Benno Wundshammer, *Windjammer-treffen* (Gerhard Stalling Verlag Oldenburg, 1972; available in English)

—, —, *Heis Die Segel!* (Gerhard Stalling Verlag, Oldenburg, 1974)

—, —, *Windjammer Parade, 1972–1978* (Gerhard Stalling Verlag Oldenburg, 1978)

Koldeway, Captain, *Jagt Grønland* (first German Arctic expedition in 1868; Stalling-Verlag, Oldenburg)

Nordon, Peter, *Die Grosse Parade der Windjammer* (Verlag F. A. Herbig, Munich)

Paschburg, Captain Hartmut, and Bock, Bruno, *Sea Cloud: Die Story eines eleganten Luxusseglers* (Koehler, 1980)

Prager, H. G., *Johann M. K. Blumenthal* (1975; also published privately as *75 Jahre: Reederei Johann M. K. Blumenthal Hamburg*)

von Stackelberg, Corvettenkapitän Freiherr Hans, *Rahsegler Im Rennen—Reisen und Regatten der Gorch Fock* (Verlag Duburger Flensburg, 1965)

Magazines and Periodicals

Morze (popular maritime magazine in Poland), with special reference to articles by Krzysztof Kaminski in October 1979, February 1980 and March 1980

National Geographic, 'From Baltic to Bi-centennial by Square-Rigger' featuring *Dar Pomorza*, by Kenneth Garrett, December 1976
Notices to Mariners International
Sea Breezes
Ships Monthly
The Smithsonian, 'How it Felt to Sail Back into History Aboard One of the Tall Ships', by Timothy Ehlen, September 1976; *'Juan Sebastian de Elcano'*, by the same author, June 1980
Tall Ships News (The STA Race Office)
Yachting Monthly
Yachting World
Programmes for the Tall Ships Races (The Sail Training Association Race Office)

ACKNOWLEDGMENTS

It is no exaggeration that I am deeply indebted to hundreds of people who helped me to write this book and it is obviously impossible to name them all, grateful as I am; but without the assistance and advice of the following organisations and individuals my task would have been impossible.

First of all my thanks to all those with whom I was invited to sail, for kind and generous hospitality, and to all the ships, captains, officers, crews, cadets and trainees who participated in the Cutty Sark Tall Ships Races, 1980, many of whom are of course mentioned in the text; I do not therefore single them out individually but I am nevertheless most grateful to them all.

Next, to the organisers of the races, the Sail Training Association and all its officers, particularly the Race Director, Mr John Hamilton, have all been tireless in providing information and checking facts. Nor do I forget Messrs Berry Brothers and Rudd Ltd, the makers of Cutty Sark Scots Whisky, who help to finance the races which are named after that delicious beverage. Their publicity controller, Mr Oliver Pemberton, was particularly helpful. The American Sail Training Association and its President, Mr Barclay Warburton III, provided vital information about the 1980 races which they organised on the other side of, and across, the Atlantic.

The following organisations and groups (and of course their officers) have all eased my task in garnering facts: the British Kiel Yacht Club; Clipper, Deutsches Jugendwerk zur See eV; Coiste An Asgard, Eire; the Directorate for Maritime Education, Copenhagen; Deutsches Schiffahrtsmuseum, Bremerhaven; the

Ecuadorian Government; Het Zeilend Zeeschip, *Eendracht*; Federal German Navy; the Merchant Navy Academy, Gdynia; Helly-Hansen (UK) Ltd; the Island Cruising Club (where I learned sailing and seamanship); the Joint Services Sailing Centre at Gosport; the Kiel Pilots Choir; the London Sailing Project; Mariners International; the National Maritime Museum, Greenwich; the Ocean Youth Club; the Polish Yachting Association; the Promenade Bookshop, Cheltenham; the Royal Artillery Yacht Club; the Royal Danish Navy; the Royal Netherlands Navy, the Royal Swedish Navy and the Royal Navy; the London Science Museum Library; Schiffergilde Bremerhaven eV; the Sea Cadet Corps; the Scheldeloodsenkoor of Flushing; *Ships Monthly* (for use of extracts from articles published); the Square Rigger Club; the Swedish Cruising Association; the Baltic Division of training ships for the Fisheries Service of the USSR; the United States Naval Academy. And my thanks to all the organising committees, staff and harbour masters, and citizens at all the ports visited by the tall ships, especially with reference in 1980, at Kristiansand, Kiel, Karlskrona, Frederikshavn and Amsterdam, for the efficiency at these harbours and for the warm and generous welcomes.

For individual reasons I must include: Erik Abranson, Commodore L. Ahrén, Cmdr W. S. B. Anderson of the Royal Yachting Association, Finn Bergmann, Mrs Janka Bielak, Herbert Boehm, Mrs Jo Brigham, Rogilio Cespedes, Captain W. P. Coolhaas, RNLS (Retd), Malcolm Darch, Maldwin Drummond DL, JP, Professor Dr Daniel Duda, Cmdr L. L. R. Foster, RN (Retd), Cmdr Sten Gattberg, RSWN, Cmdr A. H. Godwin, RN (Retd), Hennig Goes, Captain G. W. T. Griffiths, Stan Hugill, Dr T. Huitema, Mr Krzysztof Kaminski (photographer), Cmdr Olav D. Kongevold, RNN (Retd), Mr John Marriner, Mr W. H. Masefield, Mr Tsuneo Nakamura (marine photographer), Nancy Richardson, Roger Robinson, Mr J. T. Roome (Water Transport Section, Science Museum), Commodore Ø. Schau (Christian Radich-Østlandets Skoleskib), Mr Russell Self, Captain Kjell Thorsen, RNN, Mr Cornelius Vanderstar, Mr Alan Villiers, Cmdr Robert Wall, RN (Retd), Torsten Wikström and R. M. Willoughby.

For photographs I am much indebted to many people for the loan of material, and particularly to D. J. Benstead, the Official Photographer for the STA in 1980, Mrs Janka Bielak, Mr Malcolm Darch, Hennig Goes (Seestadt Bremerhaven), Deutsches Schiffahrtsmuseum, Manfred Hövener, Mr Henryk Kabat, and all other owners of copyright pictures mentioned in the captions. The quality of some of the photographs suffered unavoidably, owing to the circumstances under which they were taken. They have been included because of their interesting subject-matter.

I also thank Mrs Diana Chambers for her skill in copy-editing my typescript.

I deeply appreciate the helpful enthusiasm of my late Papa, Willie Hollins, and of my mother, Judy, who always encouraged me in all my adventures.

H.H.

INDEX

Page numbers in *italic* type refer to illustrations

Abraham Rydberg, 60; Rydberg Foundation, 31, 60
Albatros, 105, 160, 168, *89*
Albert Leo Schlageter, 53, 177; *see also Sagres II*
American Sail Training Association, 11, 14, 154, 158, 165; logo, 154, *158*; officials, 11, 63; Races, 11–24, 82, 165; results, 18, 21
Amerigo Vespucci, 149, 158, 174, *148*, *155*, *161*
Amphitrite, 45, 105, 170, *52*
Amsterdam, 8, 98, 123, 128, 138, 139, 141, 144, 145, 147, 149–159, *152*, *155*, *156*, *157*, *161*
Anna Rosa, 90, 168
Arntsen, Capt Nils, 28, 55, 167, 178, *111*
Asgard II, 160
Astarte, 67, 160, 163, 168, *68*, *162*
Amory, Lord, 36
Armas, Capt Nelson, 18, 64, 112, 167, 176, *63*
Astral, 14, 22, 80, 82
Atene, 101–2, 168
Athena, 98, 172
Avalanche, 35, 92, 100, 172

BBC (*World About Us* series), 31, 40
Baranowski, Krzysztof, 51, 112, 147, 167, 177
Beatrix, Queen of the Netherlands, 153, *151*
Belle Poule, 75, 90, 92, 95, 98, 105, 111, 114, 115, 131, 139, 154, 159, 170, 179, 180, 181, *57*, *111*, *126*, *161*
Benstead, D. J., 42
Bentsen, Capt Otto, 55, 69, 70, 76, 79, 84, 97, 106, 167, 175, *107*
Bergmann, Finn, 66
Berry Brothers and Rudd Ltd, 154
Bielak, Janka, 102, 150, *102*
Blanca Estela, 11, 18, 21, 24, 64, 82, 85, 92, 95, 100, 112, 149, 153, 159, 172, *20*, *63*
Blohm and Voss, 53, 69, 132, 175, 176, 177, 178
Blue Sirius, 71

Bockelmann, Gunther, 67, 105, 160
Bornholm, Denmark, 9, 76, 77, 79, 101
Bremerhaven, 10, 37, 55, 67, 88, 120, 159, 160, 165, *38*, *52*, *89*, *120*, *162*, *163*; history, 159—60; officials, 160
British Kiel Yacht Club, 35–6, 100
British Soldier, 46, 71, 100, 106, 149, 153, 172, *100*
Burnham, Lord, 97, 106, 149, 150, *102*

Camper and Nicholson, 15, 45, 46, 105, 108, 174
Captains: *see under individual ships' names and* Appendix A
Carillion of Wight, 102, 125, 150, 172, *182*
Carl-Gustav, King of Sweden, 111, 115
Carola, 50–1, 98, 100, 112, 128, 139, 160, 168
Cartagena, 11, 12
Cemm, Lt-Col Roger, 35
Centurion, 35, 67, 179
Cereola, 42, 82, 100, 115, 131, 139, 170
Chaser, 11, 12, 18, 182
Christiania, 128, 139, 153, 168
Christian Radich, 14, 15, 18, 21, 25, 28, 63, 75, 108, 174, 179, 180, 181, 182, *14*
Christian Venturer, 11, 14, 18, 21, 64, 128, 153, 159, 168
Chwan, 64, 98, 172
Classes A and B, definitions, 12
Clipper Deutsches Jugendwerk zur See eV, 88, 104–5, 168, 169, 170, *52*
Colin Archer, 128, 139, 141, 153, 168; Sailing Club (Seilskoyteklubben Colin Archer), 128
Creidne, 144, 150, 172
Creole, 15, 16, 46, 82, 87, 98–9, 118, 123, 139, 141, 147, 167, 174, *13*, *17*, *156*
Crew exchange, 110–11, 115–22
Cruise-in-company, 34, 110–11, 115–22

Cutty Sark, 76
Cutty Sark (whisky co), 144, 153, 154; *see also* Tall Ships Races
Cutty Sark Friendship Trophy, 63, 64, *63*
Cutty Sark Trophy, 58, 98, 153–4, *151*

Danish Government, 55, 69, 75, 93, 104
Danish Merchant Navy, 56, 69, 73–4, 76, 92, 93
Danmark, 14–15, 22, 55, 57, 66, 69–99, 104–109, 123, 167, 174–5, 179, 181, *42*, *71*, *72*, *77*, *81*, *83*, *85*, *94*, *96*, *99*, *104*, *107*, *109*, *113*
Dannebrog, 123, 135, *125*
Dark Horse, 98, 128, 172
Dar Pomorza, 66, 70–1, 75, 77, 82, 85, 87, 90, 95, 98, 105, 111–12, 115, 123, 128, 131–47, 153, 158, 160, 164, 165, 167, 175, 181, 182, *41*, *78*, *99*, *111*, *124*, *129*, *130*, *133*, *134*, *136*, *137*, *138*, *140*, *142*, *143*, *145*, *146*, *147*, *151*, *152*, *156*, *157*
Dasher, 46, 71, 100, 115, 141, 149, 153, 172, 182
Deutsches Schiffahrtsmuseum, 67, 159, 160
Dione, 98, 170
Direktoratet for Søfartsuddannelsen, Copenhagen, *see Danmark*; Danish Government
Donald Searle, 36, 85, 95, 122, 170, *34*
Doris II, 128, 172
Duet, 127, 179, 180, 182, *126*
Duke of Edinburgh, 108
Dusmarie, 87, 88, 115, 141, 168, 182, *89*

Eagle, 14, 53, 70, 175
Eendracht, 48, 50, 66, 82, 84, 128, 156, 158, 170, *155*
Elinor, 64, 95, 101, 168, *68*, *92*
Ellida, 98, 168
El Pirata, 14, 22, 32, 88, 90, 131, 144, 150, 160, 170, *89*
Engel, Capt Hans, 55, 104, *62*

Equinoxe, 98, 114, 168
Esmeralda, 21, 175
Esperanza, 12
Etoile, 75, 90, 92, 95, 98, 105,
    111, 114, 115, 131, 139, 141,
    153, 159, 170, 179, 180, 57,
    111, 161

Falken, 35, 57–8, 66, 75, 82, 85,
    95, 102, 104, 114, 122, 131, 153,
    159, 170, 179, 180, 181, 182, 59
Falmouth, 35, 67, 76, 108, 154,
    165, 179
Falster, 9, 35, 69, 70
'Family', the, 61, 153
Fårö, 85, 87, 88, 90
'Father', 61, 63, 153, 62; see also
    Howard, Greville
Federal German Navy, 14, 53,
    55, 176
Flamingo, 35, 92, 100, 170
Flying Clipper, 60
Flying 'P' Line, 37, 120
Fortuna II, 12
Frederikshavn, 8, 34, 79, 93, 110,
    111, 115, 122, 123; history, 122,
    126

Gattberg, Cdr Sten, 58, 98
GB II, 36, 48, 64, 110
Gdansk Shipyard, 51, 177
Gdynia, 53, 65, 66, 75, 87, 132,
    164, 165, 181
Georg Stage, 28, 55–7, 75, 77, 79,
    82, 87, 90, 92–4, 95, 98, 111,
    115, 167, 176, 44, 91, 111, 116
Germania Shipyard, 39, 177, 178
German Maritime Museum, 67,
    159, 160
Gladan, 57, 58, 98, 154, 180, 181,
    182, 59
Glad Tidings, 12
Gloria, 11, 18, 165, 176
Goes, Hennig, 160
Gorch Fock I, 53, 55, 75, 85, 178,
    54, see also Tovarisch
Gorch Fock II, 14, 18, 21, 43, 53,
    55, 63–4, 69, 73, 75, 77, 82, 85,
    90, 95, 97, 98, 104, 123, 131,
    135, 138, 139, 141, 144, 147,
    150, 153, 160, 167, 176, 179,
    180, 181, 182, 54, 80, 96, 113,
    161, 162
Gosport, 12, 36, 46, 67, 100, 127,
    174
Gotland, 9, 79, 82, 84, 85, 87, 92
Gratia of Gothenburg, 46, 58, 60,
    61, 64, 67, 84, 105, 112, 160,
    168, 47
Gratitude of Gothenburg, 46, 58,
    60, 61, 64, 67, 84, 88, 105, 112,
    160, 165, 168, 182, 47, 112, 164
Gre 14, 128, 168
Grønland, 67, 105, 160, 163, 66,
    162
Guayas, 11, 18, 21, 24, 43, 45,
    64, 76, 77, 82, 85, 92, 95, 98,
    105, 112, 123, 138, 139, 141,

147, 150, 153, 159, 165, 167,
    176, 19, 23, 63, 104, 155

Hajduk, 65, 92, 114, 128, 153,
    172
Halcyon, 84, 131, 170, 180, 181,
    182, 90
Hamilton, John, 16, 37, 43, 45,
    48, 105, 106, 108, 110, 111, 150,
    153, 109, 151
Hansen, Capt Knud, 70, 76, 77,
    108
Hansen, Capt Wilhelm, 15, 70,
    76, 77, 175
Hetman, 65, 92, 128, 141, 172,
    182
Holtenauer Lotsenchor
    Knurrhahn, 43, 61
Horst Wessel, 53, 69, 70, 175;
    see also Eagle
Hoshi, 45, 46, 84, 94, 98, 115,
    131, 168, 179, 180, 45
Hövener, Capt Manfred, 67,
    163, 168, 162
Howard, Lt Cdr The Hon
    Greville, 7, 22, 61, 63, 100, 102,
    105, 111, 114, 115, 150, 153, 62,
    125, 151; see also 'Father'
Hugill, Stan, 31, 39, 40, 32
Hussar, 28, 39, 177

IJmuiden, 58, 141, 145, 147, 149,
    161, 181
Illingworth, John, 46, 108, 127
Illingworth, Admiral Juan, 18
Iron Shackle Fraternity, 53, 177;
    see also Pogoria
Isis, 92, 98, 172
Island Cruising Club, 45, 46, 60,
    168
Italian Navy, 149, 174

James, David, 127
Jarramas, 58, 75
Jens Krogh, 82, 128, 139, 168
Jespersen, Capt B. Barner, 55–7,
    167, 176, 111
Ji Fung, 160, 165
Joana I, 131, 139, 159, 170
Joint Services Sailing Centre, 12,
    46, 100–1, 172, 173
Jolie Brise, 87, 128, 131, 168, 182
Joseph Conrad, 56, 93–4, 160
Juan Sebastian de Elcano, 12, 21,
    176, 177
Jurkiewicz, Extra-Master
    Kazimierz, 133, 175, 137

Kanaloa, 128, 150, 170
Karlskrona, 35, 42, 58, 61, 64,
    67, 70, 71, 75, 84, 95, 96–116,
    117, 131, 139, 153, 96, 101, 109,
    111, 112, 113, 116; committee
    and officials, 64, 97, 105;
    history, 97
Karstensens Skibvaerft, 61, 160,
    165, 164
Kiel, 24, 31, 35–70, 100, 101,

104, 106, 110, 132, 153, 177,
    178; history, 43; Official
    Committee, 43, 45; Pilots
    Choir, 43, 61
Kinau, Johann, 53, 55, 160
Kranich, 35, 64, 100, 114, 170
Kristiansand, 10, 11, 14, 15,
    18–28, 31, 55, 58, 63, 75, 178,
    180, 20; history, 22
Kruzenshtern, 37, 43, 73, 75, 76,
    77, 82, 87, 90, 95, 98, 111,
    115–23, 139, 141, 147, 150, 154,
    158–60, 167, 177, 182, 38,
    78, 111, 116, 117, 120, 121, 155,
    163

Laeisz Flying 'P' Line, 37, 120,
    177
Latvian Shipping Company, 85
La Vague, 79, 80
Leader of Gothenburg, 46, 60, 160,
    182, 47
Ledina, 128, 139, 141, 168
Leningrad Marine Engineering
    College, 85, 172
Le Papillon, 70, 84, 90, 144, 147,
    150, 159, 169
Liaison officers, 43, 58, 98, 128,
    150
Lindø, 11–12, 18, 20–1, 24, 63–4,
    159, 169
Lindormen, 76
Lisbon, 46, 70, 106, 108, 165,
    179
Liv, 128, 139, 153, 169
London Sailing Project, 36, 37,
    42, 48, 64, 110, 34

Mabel Stevens, 12
Magdalene Vinnen II, 122, 178
Malcolm Miller, 50, 82, 110, 125,
    139, 160, 170, 180, 181, 103, 126
Margrethe, Queen of Denmark,
    55, 123, 125
Mariners International, 22, 30–2,
    88, 90, 165, 29, 89
Maritime Trust, 46
Marques, 31, 32, 182
Marriner, John, 106
Martin, Capt John, 21,112, 63
Master Builder, 125, 127, 182
Medea, 98, 172
Mircea II, 53, 178
Mitzlaff-Laiesz, Frau Christine
    von, 163
Mjojo, 128, 169
Morgan, Bernard, 7, 43, 46
Morning Watch, 106
Mountbatten, Earl, 46
Moyana, 84, 179
Myatt, Lt Col James, 37, 48, 64,
    106–8, 110–11

Najaden, 58, 75
Nakskov Shipyard, 69, 70, 71,
    132, 175
Niobe, 53
Norfolk, Virginia, 12

Norwegian Maritime Museum, Oslo, 28, 128
Nyborg Søfartsskole, 16, 167

Ocean Youth Club, 100, 110, 125–7, 160, 171
Olaf, King of Norway, 22
Öland, 9, 82, 95
Olechnowicz, Capt Tadeusz, 98, 112, 133, 135, 143, 145, 147, 153, 167, 175, *111*, *137*, *151*
Olifant von Wedel, 87, 98, 160, 169, *86*
Opsail, 14
Öquist, Lt Cdr Claes, 58, 98
Østlandets Skoleskibs, 14, 174
Ostseehalle, 63, 64
Outlaw, West Germany, 131, 160, 169

Padua, 37, 120, 159, 177, *163*; see also Kruzenshtern
Pamir, 53, 104
Parades of Sail, 10, 12, 14, 62, 64, 65–9, 70, 88, 104, 106, 115–17, 132, 141, 145, 149, 159, 160, *10*, *38*, *52*, *55*, *89*, *116*, *161*, *162*
Perevozchikov, Capt Alexey B., 118, 122, 159, 167, 177, *111*, *163*
Peter von Danzig, 100, 131, 141, 153, 171
Phelan, Carl, 40, 118, *117*
Phelan, Capt Chris, 37, 40, 84, *90*
Phoenix, 31, 32, 182
Pogoria, 51, 53, 66, 75, 77, 82, 85, 92, 95, 98, 112, 115, 123, 128, 135, 138, 139, 141, 144, 145, 153, 154, 160, 167, 177, *52*, *116*
Polish Yachting Association, 65, 66
Polonez, 51
Pride of Baltimore, 12, 21
Prince Berthil of Sweden, 111, 112, 114, 115, 117, *112*
Prinzess Eitel Friedrich, 132, 175; see also Dar Pomorza
Prize-giving: Amsterdam, 98, 150, 153, *151*; Karlskrona, 95, 111, 112, 114, *111*, *112*; Kiel, 63, 64, *63*
Provident, 46, 60, 180, *47*

Queen, 82, 85, 92, 95, 112, 114, 172

Radio communications, 22, 24, 42, 71, 73, 74, 79, 80, 82, 84, 85, 90, 98, 106, 108, 118, 138, 139, 144–5, 147
Ramrod, 82, 153, 171, 172
Ran, 128, 150, 171
Ritza, 85, 92, 114, 139, 172, 182
Rona, 36, 179, 180, 181, 182
Royal Armoured Corps, 12
Royal Artillery: Regiment, 48, 100, 106, 110–11, 153; Yacht

Club, 106
Royal Corps of Signals, 12
Royal Danish Navy, 73, 76, 93, 122
Royalist, 35, 67, 69, 73, 84, 95, 101, 115, 118, 131, 138, 139, 144, 150, 160, 169, *68*, *86*, *119*
Royal Navy, 12, 46, 69, 100–1, 153
Royal Netherlands Navy, 48, 150; see also Urania
Royal Norwegian Navy, 25
Royal Swedish Navy, 57–8, 82, 97, 98, 114–15; see also Falken and Gladan
Roztocze, 65, 98, 128, 172, *100*
Russian Fisheries Service, 37, 117, 120, 177–8
RYA/DTI Certificates, 36, 37, 46, 48, 101, 110

Sabre, 11, 12, 15, 18, 46, 95, 100, 112, 139, 141, 173, 181, 182, *13*, *101*
Sagres II, 53, 177
Sail Amsterdam, 149–59, *152*, *155*, *156*, *157*, *161*; Official Committee, 150, 153
Sailing ships, advantages for training, 56–7
Sail Training Association, 14, 21, 40, 42, 45, 46, 48, 50, 53, 55, 58, 61, 62, 64, 66, 69, 70, 87, 97, 98, 102, 106, 108–11, 115, 123, 126, 131, 132, 141, 150, 153, 154, 158, 159, 160; statistics, 63, 160
St Barbara, 48, 106
St Barbara II, 100, 173, 181
Samuel Whitbread, 127, 181, *126*
Sampo, 169
Schiffergilde Bremerhaven, 67, 69
Scholfield, Col. R., 21, 48, 154
Scott, Morin, 35, 67, 69, 84, 118, 169
Sea Cadet Corps, 35, 36, 67, 69, 160
Sea Cloud, 28, 38, 39, 60, 67, 76, 77, 79, 82, 98, 138, 149, 158, 177, *155*
Sedov, 122, 165, 178
Sepha Vollaars, 128, 171
Seute Deern: barque, 160; ketch, 90, 104, 169
Shanties, 24, 31, 39, 40, 43, 50, 61, 67, 158, 160
Simon Bolivar, 18, 165
Sir Winston Churchill, 50, 82, 108, 110, 123, 141, 147, 160, 171, 179, 180, 181, 182, *110*, *126*
Skagen, 8, 31, 61, 125, 132, 145, 160, 165
Smith, Martin, 31, *29*
Smith, Mike, *120*
Somerset, 40, 42, 45, 48, 64, 71, 79, 82, 84, 90, 95, 98, 105, 139, 144, 145, 150, 153, *90*; crew, 40,

105, 153, *42*
Sørlandet, 11, 24–33, 37, 39, 40, 43, 55, 66, 73, 75, 76, 77, 79, 82, 90, 95, 98, 111, 123, 139, 141, 147, 153, 160, 167, 178, 179, 180, *10*, *26*, *27*, *29*, *30*, *32*, *33*, *40*, *41*, *59*, *99*, *152*
Sparta, 85, 114, 115, 147, 173
Spencer Thetis Wharf, Cowes, 16, 17
Spirit of Adventure, 165
Square-Rigger Club, 69
Stadtbildstelle Seestadt Bremerhaven, 55, 88, 163
Stormvogel, 127, 128, 159, 173
Svanen of Stockholm, 94, 95, 98, 150, 159, 169
Svenska Kryssarklubbens Seglarskola (Swedish Cruising Association), 46, 58, 60–1, 105, 112, 160, 165, 168, 182
Symfoni, 105, 115, 128, 173

Tall Ships Races: **1956** 16, 18, 43, 46, 58, 60, 84, 108, 123, 160, 179; **1960** 55, 179; **1962** 55, 106, 179; **1964** 70, 106, 108, 179; **1966** 35, 67, 108, 179, 180; **1968** 31, 55, 58, 180; **1970** 46, 80, 180; **1972** 43, 58, 62, 104, 132, 145, 181, 181; **1974** 31, 61, 65, 87, 132, 154, 181; **1975** 58, 181, 182; **1976** 13, 21, 31, 32, 36, 42, 48, 51, 55, 58, 64, 65, 67, 70, 80, 85, 98, 110, 120, 123, 132, 137, 149, 154, 182; **1977** 58, 115, 182; **1978** 14, 22, 31, 32, 51, 52, 55, 58, 60, 61, 65, 75, 85, 97, 98, 102, 127, 131, 132, 149, 154, 182; **1979** 22, 102, 182; **1980** (Cutty Sark), 144, 151, 153, 154; logo, 144, 154, *158*; Race Office, 40, 42, 45, 48, 95; results see Appendix A and Prize-giving; rules and conditions of entry, 12, 22, 39; statistics, 63
Tawau, 106, 108, 179
Tecklenborg, J. C., 37, 120, 163, 177
Tenerife, 55, 78, 110, 111, 120, 133, 180, 182, *13*
The Great Escape, 128, 171
Theodora, 127, 180
Thorsen, Capt Kjell, 14, 174
Tielsa, 128, 173
Tina IV, 67, 171
Tineke, 128, 171
Tovarisch, 53, 55, 85, 178, 181, 182, *54*
Tryglaw, 65, 115, 128, 173

Unicorn, 12
United States Coast Guard, 14, 39, 53, 69, 70, 175
United States Naval Academy, 14, 22, 82
Urania, 48, 82, 92, 98, 100, 115,

128, 150, 173, 179, 180, 181, 182, *49*, *129*, *151*

Vanderstar, Cornelius, 22, 80, 82
Varuna, 160
Villiers, Alan, 75, 88, 93, 160
Vira, 16, 174; *see also Creole*
Visborg, 115
Visby, 9, 82, 84

Walross III, 64, 92, 95, 98, 112, 115, 131, 149, 159, 173
Warburton III, Barclay, 11; *see*

also American Sail Training Association
Westblad, Lt Ragnar, 57–8, 104, 114, 122, 170, *59*
West German Navy, *see* Federal German Navy
Wind, Capt Horst, 55, 63–4, 167, 176
Windjammer Parades, *see* Parades of Sail
Wodnik II, 65, 128
Wojewoda Pomorski, 65, 92, 98, 115, 128, 139, 173

Wollter, Kjell, 58, 60–1, 88, 105, 112, 168, *112*
World About Us (BBC series), 31, 40
Wyższa Szkoła Morska (Merchant Navy Academy), Gdynia, 132–3, 165, 167, 175; *see also Dar Pomorza*

Young America, 12

Zebu, 64, 71, 171
Zenobe Gramme, 14, 22, 154
Zew Morza, 51, 128, 139, 141, 158, 171